HEFNER'S GONNA KILL ME WHEN HE READS THIS...

HEFNER'S GONNA KILL ME WHEN HE READS THIS...

By
Stephen Byer

Allen-Bennett, Inc. / Chicago / 1972

Library of Congress Catalog Card Number: 77-188440
ISBN: 0-88260-280-2

To my wife and three sons, and to my editor, Robert Tamarkin—all of whom should be roundly applauded for their willingness to accept that which Huf couldn't.

CONTENTS

A CAST OF CHARACTERS

Hugh M. Hefner — *Chairman of the Board of Directors, President and Editor-Publisher*

Robert S. Preuss — *Executive Vice President*

Glenn L. Hefner — *Vice President, Treasurer*

Auguste C. Spectorsky — *Senior Vice President, Associate Publisher and Editorial Director*

Arnold J. Morton — *Senior Vice President, Director of Club-Hotel Division*

Victor A. Lownes — *Vice President, International Division, and Director of Creative Development*

Henri Lorenzi — *Director of Operations, Hotels and Clubs*

Arthur Paul — *Vice President, Art Director*

Howard Lederer — *Vice President, Media Sales*

Nelson Futch — *Vice President, Promotion*

John Mastro — *Vice President, Production*

Edward A. Rogers — *Vice President, Entertainment*

Richard S. Rosenzweig — *Vice President, Executive Assistant to the President*

Robert A. Gutwillig — *Vice President, Publishing Development*

Lee Gottlieb — *Vice President, Public Relations*

Lance Hooper — *Vice President, Finance*

Theo Frederick — *Director of Personnel*

Alvin Teller — *Director of Corporate Development*

Morton Pollock — *Promotion Manager*

And the Bit Players

Author's Note: Most of the above corporate titles were different than the ones used while I was at Playboy. The change in titles was the result of a reorganization Playboy underwent in February of 1971. While the titles may have changed, the names have not, nor have characters.

PROLOGUE

It was the summer of '55. My lovely Heide lay stretched out before me in all her glorious, womanly splendor. Her long raven hair fell freely across her soft, tan shoulders and her flowing limbs, seductively poised, projected wanton tenderness. Oh, how those shapely, full breasts and velvet loins filled me with an airy aphrodisiac, sending my body and mind quivering with what seemed to be an insatiable desire. She spoke not a word. Nor I. We lay there together in my bed. Was a 13-year-old boy capable of handling this luscious creature, five years his senior? She was mine for the taking. Oh, Heide, Heide, Heide . . .

Thus my very first encounter with the Playmate in the *Playboy* magazine had ended all too briefly. The fantasy of youth had sent me billowing into a blissful euphoria. It also sent me masturbating into the magazine's centerfold.

I never dreamed then that fourteen years later I would become an integral part of the Playboy machine, churning out the stuff that feeds the fantasies of millions of others.

I guess one of my assets has always been a basic forthright-ness when it comes to dealing with people (if you read the Psychological Evaluation, perhaps you will gather that), whether in business or in my private life. If I think someone is right, I'll applaud. If he's wrong, I'll boo. In retrospect, it is probably this very quality that led me to buck heads with my former employer, one Hugh Marston Hefner, founder-editor-publisher of *Playboy* magazine, the hub of what many people consider to be the most successful publishing entity in U.S. history.

Perhaps the questions most commonly asked me in the year I worked for Playboy, and since I left, are: "What is Playboy really like?" and "How could you leave Playboy?" The answer I give sums it up: "What Playboy is really like is why I was able to walk away from a $200,000 vice presidency at age 28 without any qualms."

One of my close friends knew I was writing this book and asked me why I thought I was qualified to do it. I told him, "The gauntlet has fallen to me because there is no one else to accept it; because I experienced it and came out with my brains unscrambled enough to relate what happened."

My experiences at Playboy were sometimes interesting, sometimes funny, sometimes disgusting, but always illuminating. That's why I'm sharing the story with the public, a vast part of which has been curious for many years about what *really* goes on inside the $130-million Playboy empire.

There are, of course, personal reasons, too, such as the satisfaction of being recognized as successful in my line of business at a relatively young age, and the material reward, or in capitalistic vernacular, money. But the first reason is most important to me. Why, as a budding author I might even get a crack at the Dick Cavett show! Who knows what doors will open—or close.

Regardless, it's a story worth telling, even if Hefner is gonna kill me when he reads it!

Stephen Byer
May 1972

(FROM THE FILES OF PLAYBOY)

PSYCHOLOGICAL EVALUATION

STEPHEN B. BYER

PLAYBOY

PSYCHOLOGICAL EVALUATION

STEPHEN B. BYER

PLAYBOY

According to your request, we have interviewed and
tested Mr. Byer, and we are submitting in confidence
our professional opinion concerning his qualifications
as Director of Mail Marketing for Playboy.

Mr. Byer is an exceptionally talented man, but he is
also a highly individualistic one. He is not well-
suited for corporate life; basically, he is in business
for himself. He will not be contained within an organization for long; either he will be given a free hand to
operate as he pleases — and also be given a ''piece of
the action'' to reward him for results — or he will
precipitate conflict, test the limits of authority,
and eventually find some reason to justify his leaving.
He is a self-serving person who is indifferent to the
needs of other people. He feels little compunction
in steamrolling those who get in his way. One can
anticipate his making enemies in the organization.

One can also expect him to achieve results — perhaps
dramatic results, as he puts his brains and guts and
drive to work. He may not remain with Playboy for a
long period of time, but he will make a definite
impact as long as he is employed by your organization.

Specifically, we may summarize his strengths and
limitations as follows:

ASSETS	LIABILITIES
Very quick, bright, and shrewd	Self-centered
	Contemptuous of others
Knowledgeable in his field	A poor ''team player''
	Impulsive and sometimes
Enterprising and resourceful	superficial in his thinking
A keen instinct for the	Difficult, if not

jugular
Extremely aggressive
Unusual drive and energy
Resolute in his behavior
A strong, dominant per-
  sonality
Articulate
Goal-oriented
An achiever — at all
  costs, perhaps, but
  definitely an achiever

impossible to
  contain
Opportunistic
Temperamental
Little loyalty to any-
  one other than himself
Materialistic and
  acquisitive

Mr. Byer is now 27 years of age. He was born and
raised in Chicago where his father, a pharmacist,
provided his family with an upper-middle class standard
of living as long as he owned his own drug store; he
is now earning a more moderate income, as he sold the
store and works for another pharmacist. Mr. Byer has
two sisters. One, four years older than himself, has
her master's degree in microbiology; her husband has
his Ph.D. His other sister, four years younger than
himself, graduated summa cum laude from college and is
now studying at the graduate level at the University
of Jerusalem.

He graduated in the top third of his class from the
Oak Park High School in June of 1958. He played on the
junior varsity football team, but otherwise failed to
distinguish himself in high school. Next he attended
the University of Illinois at Champaign for one academic year as an art student. He then returned to
Chicago, where he worked full-time during the day while
attending Northwestern at night as a student in liberal
arts. Two years later he went back to Champaign as a
part-time student in the school of journalism; he held
a full-time job outside of school. He dropped out of
the university in June of 1963 after completing an
estimated 4-5ths of the courses required for a degree;
he specifically plans not to complete his undergraduate
schooling and obtain a bachelor's degree.

He has never served on active duty in the armed forces;
he was classified 1-Y because of an ulcer developed at
the age of 17. He left Champaign in June of 1963 to
join Cowles Communications in Des Moines as a direct
mail copywriter. He rose rapidly in the organization

during his four and one-half years with Cowles; at the
time of his departure in November of 1967, he was
general manager of the Contract Services Division —
a division which he had largely developed on his own.
At this point he joined forces with his wife's uncle,
Al Sloan, in a direct mail consulting firm called
Whitney-Forbes, Inc.; Mr. Byer owned a twenty percent
equity in this business. The firm — and Mr. Byer —
prospered mightily during his two years with the
organization. But he left in September of this year,
after a dispute with Mr. Sloan; he subsequently
joined your organization as director of mail marketing.

In August of 1964 he married a Chicago girl who graduated from the University of Illinois with an education
degree. They now have two sons, 30 and 4 months of
age. They are renting a twelve-room apartment at
1 East Schiller for $1,000 per month. The Byers drive
a '69 Cadillac and a '51 MG-TD. Mr. Byer estimates
his current net worth at $400,000 — including $250,000
in such non-liquid assets as personal belongings and
objets d'art.

Outside of work he spends most of his time at home
with the family or walking his Irish Wolfhound. He is
very interested in art, as he shops the galleries and
collects paintings and objects of interest to him. He
is also highly interested in photography, archeology,
and reading. He is not one to take part in athletic
activities, other than shoot a game of pool at the
table he has in his apartment. He reports that his
health is very good at this time; his weight is down
to 212 pounds from 234. He never smokes and never
drinks, according to his self-report. He needs little
sleep to maintain his high energy level.

He is very superior to the general population in terms
of native mental ability, and quite superior to the
average college graduate. He is a quick-witted fellow
who has the mental initiative, not only to size up a
situation, but to take direct, immediate action on the
basis of his observations. He both sees and seizes
opportunities; he may commit many more sins of commission than the next fellow, but far fewer sins of
omission. He is imaginative and innovative.

While he is reportedly well-grounded and highly knowl-
edgeable in his field, he is much more likely to operate on sudden insight and intuition than facts and
logic. Like many gamblers, he is a superstitious
fellow who indulges in cliche thinking. Of course he
can be highly intellectual when he chooses – and even
affect a contemplative, philosophical mien – but he is
by nature more the doer than the thinker.

He has tremendous energies which he is fully prepared
to invest in his work. He can attack a problem with
lots of enthusiasm – in fact, with feverish intensity.
He has all sorts of drive and determination. As he
stated in his own words: ''I am resolute, and I will
not be deterred from a set course of action.'' He
aggressively seeks out what he wants; he is not one to
sit back and wait for good fortune to come his way.

He is an egotist – from the initials embroidered on
his shirt cuff to the self-centered demands he makes
on other people. He expects more of them than he is
prepared to give in return. He would let others, for
example, invest the risk capital, but he would then
demand the lion's share of any subsequent profits. In
all his dealings, Mr. Byer is always looking out for
his own best interests. Not unexpectedly, he is very
moralistic in his pronouncements, as he strives to
justify whatever he does in self-righteous terms.

This man is a master of many roles. He can be a
pleasant, smiling, friendly fellow; he can be an enthusiastic ''pitch'' man; he can be a soft-spoken, delib-
erate academic type; he can be a hard-nosed, tough-
minded executive, dealing with others in a no-nonsense
manner; and he can be extremely hostile, cynical, and
sarcastic toward others. Basically, he is insensitive
to the needs of fellow man; he will try to manipulate
others to suit his purposes. He is especially con-
temptuous of those whom he considers weak; as he
stated on item No. 55 of the Sentence Completion Form:
''I don't like men who/are weak – physically or emotionally.'' He will always try to establish himself as a
dominant party in any relationship.

He is a grandstander who wants to look spectacular on
every play. With his strong need to be the standout

star, he hardly fits comfortably into a team effort.
Supremely self-confident, he will put other people
down — much to their dismay. He has had a history of
personality clashes — which, of course, have always
been the other fellow's fault.

Mr. Byer is a prima donna who will expect special
treatment and privileges. He will do what he wants
in an organization, then inform his boss. It will be
virtually impossible to supervise or control him, as
he operates on his own initiative. He is extremely independent. As he stated on item No. 29 of the Sentence
Completion Form: ''I enjoy/that which I do. I do not
do that which I don't enjoy.''

His greatest asset is his ability to get results. He
surmounts obstacles which would frustrate lesser men.
What he does is set his sights on a specific objective,
then mobilize his considerable resources to achieve it.
He is a highly motivated, goal-oriented man. As long
as his objectives, and those of the organization, are
reasonably congruent, both parties will be happy. When
they diverge — as they inevitably must — Mr. Byer will
have neither the patience nor the loyalty to subordinate his immediate interests to those of the organization. While we predict, therefore, that he and Playboy
will part company in the next few years, we also think
it is highly likely that he will make a major contribution to your organization in the interim. He may be
brash and obnoxious, but he can also be very, very
productive.

CM:pd

Chapter 1
Keeper of The Gate

A stubborn Chicago basking in an autumn sun refused to let go of summer. Green was everywhere. But where I was, it made no difference. It could just as well have been a gray, wintry day outside. A lean man dressed in yellow pajamas and an orange robe bounced up the circular staircase, breaking the silence in the encapsuled room where I had been waiting and browsing amid a clutter of books, photographs and memorabilia. He half-trotted toward me and shook my hand for the first and just about last time. He has a thing about handshaking. He doesn't like to because his hands are soft and sort of pink and pudgy and almost hairless. Hugh Marston Hefner is extremely self-conscious about his hands.

Perhaps it was the nature of this meeting that it called for informality and openness between relative strangers. After all, I was there to size up my prospective employer, and he was just as eager to find out what I was all about. I assumed Hefner had already gotten some feedback on me from the other top Playboy executives whom I had been screened by previously. And there was undoubtedly a dossier on me

19

compiled by the executive search firm Playboy had hired to find a mail order sales manager.

Any preconceived ideas I had about Hefner stemmed from myriad stories that had appeared in newspapers and national magazines, touting him as the Horatio Alger of the publishing world. There also were his TV appearances. It all added up to knowing Hefner's public image, no more, no less.

However, I had met Hefner almost 10 years earlier, in 1960, when circumstances were quite different for both of us. I was earning $130 a week as an art designer for Fuller & Smith & Ross, a Chicago advertising agency. I had started at the agency in 1959 as an $85-a-week traffic supervisor responsible for tracking down art work and various materials for the preparation of ads. The job had been my first one since quitting the University of Illinois at Champaign after my freshman year.

Despite the meager starting salary, there were many rewards for a young bachelor living on his own in Chicago. One was knowing a girl who lived in my building, a Kansas-bred beauty who worked as a dice girl at the Gaslight Club.

Occasionally she came home from the Gaslight at two or three in the morning, awakened me, and with the enthusiasm of a teenager going to the big prom, she'd say: "Hey, let's go to a party," her blue eyes sparkling. I'd drag myself out of bed, dress and go with her.

One night we ended up at the penthouse apartment of a friend of a friend's. From one corner of the smoky, overcrowded room, a rather distinguished-looking man, wearing a wry grin, walked over and said, "Excuse me, sir, but I think you have a lovely wife." The game began. "Thank you, but she's not my wife," I replied, as I think he hoped I would. "Your fiancee?" he asked. "No. We're just good friends." He asked me to introduce him and I did. I suppose it was love at first sight, because eventually those two got married.

The stately gentleman for whom I had played Cupid was Marshall Caifano, allegedly a member of a very select club generally known as the Chicago syndicate. He also was a member of another private club, although it was not nearly as selective, called the Playboy Club. Marshall was one of its earliest keyholders and was a close friend of Hefner's.

At this time the Chicago Playboy Club on Walton Street, near the posh section of Michigan Avenue, was the only one in the country. And Hefner, sitting at a circular table near the door, nodded hello to the patrons as they entered. He was 33 and already a self-made millionaire. There were clear traces that he had worked hard for it. His face was gaunt and tired-looking and he was downright skinny. His accomplishments were already becoming somewhat of a legend in the public eye. In just seven years he had built a $16-million empire. More than 1.2 million readers were buying the magazine each month at 50 cents a copy, and the smartly dressed key holders were shelling out $2 million a year at the club. He had even projected the Playboy image on television with his weekly "Playboy's Penthouse," depicting his ideas on how life ought to be lived by the young urban male. Hefner had made bosoms a big business.

But despite his growing reputation as the "Midas of the Midwest," there was still a basic modesty and integrity about him. And so to know Hugh Hefner then was merely to know the keeper of the gate of the Chicago Playboy Club.

My introduction to Hefner came through Caifano. Now, Caifano has many good and many bad traits. One of the bad was acting as an extortionist for the syndicate. (At this writing, he is serving a term in Leavenworth [Kansas] penitentiary on a 1966 conviction in California for extortion, for which he was sentenced to ten years. Concurrent with that is a twelve-year sentence for fraud, to which he pleaded guilty in 1967.)

But his good traits included a sincere desire for human relationships. So when people who saw us together assumed I was either Marshall's bastard or adopted son, as Hefner and others did, he did nothing to correct this notion. To the best of my knowledge, Caifano was not an investor in Playboy, but he took many people to the club because of his friendship with Hefner.

So here in 1969—in the solitude of a conference room in

21

Hefner's baronial mansion—we were meeting again. He showed no recollection of our acquaintanceship years earlier and I saw no reason to refresh his memory.

Changes were obvious. He was a good thirty pounds heavier and there was now roundness to his face, with its almost sallow complexion. The eyes were still dark and piercing, but the tired look had been replaced by an alert and confident expression.

Admittedly, I was a little nervous and at the same time a bit titillated. I always get a kick out of meeting celebrities, and that's exactly what Hefner had bloomed into; also the "I knew him when" thought flashed through my mind, amusing me as I remembered that at the time a Chicago gangster was the link between us.

I was also considering doing my number on him, a dazzling display of verbal footwork about past business experience, plus my ideas for direct mail hustling of keys and subscriptions and Playboy products. Doing my number is what a friend of mine calls it. "Steve, do the number on them," he'll say, "tell them about Whitney-Forbes, how you started with one client and ended up with 14, doing annual sales in the millions. And don't forget to mention Cowles, how you began their direct marketing division and today with the demise of *Look* magazine it's the only thing left in the company. Go through the number, Steve."

It's sort of fun to do. I enjoy people sitting there with a curious expression that asks, "Who is this strange fat man with the mustache, thick sideburns and blue-tinted glasses? How does he know so much about direct mail marketing?"

So I was anticipating doing that with Hefner and at the same time I was trying to anticipate his questions.

After we introduced ourselves, he said, "Well, I understand you're thinking of joining us."

"That's right," I answered.

"Is there anything you'd like to know about the organization or me?"

"Not at the moment," I shook my head. "Much of it I've discussed with some of the others."

22

"Well, then, would you mind if I asked questions?"

"By all means, go right ahead."

"Tell me," he said, "have you seen any of our current promotional efforts?"

"I've seen a couple, but only as a consumer." He wanted to know what I thought of them. I asked which specific one he had in mind and he said, "Take any of them."

"All right," I said, rather relieved, because there was one I was especially ready for launching on. "Let's start with the key sales effort, your triple gift program. I think it's an example of something that was a good idea at its inception but it's no longer either feasible or plausible."

And he asked, as I hoped, "Oh, why not?"

"Because the nature of the gifts," and now I took off, not giving him a chance to interrupt, "the LeRoy Neiman print (unframed, mediocre, cheap and rolled into a tube), the four lighter-than-air aluminum tankers and the year's subscription to *Playboy*, appeal to a class of person that you are not particularly interested in soliciting as key club members. They damage your broad purpose of acquiring for Playboy Clubs International a level of membership that is above the class that's looking for free gifts. The point I'm trying to make is that now the promotion of the key club offer is centered solely around the freebies; it says nothing vital about the clubs and hotels. I would attempt to portray them, and the other benefits of being a member of PCI, in such a way as to present the best of them graphically and in the copy."

At that point Hefner did interrupt.

"Perhaps that accounts for the reduction in key sales over the last couple of years," he said thoughtfully.

"I'm sure it does, to a large extent," I said, "and I'm sure, too, that the economy has something to do with it."

"If our promotional slant is at fault, it should be corrected." I agreed.

We then discussed not only the sales of Playboy products but the products themselves, what was in the line and why and what types of items ought to be considered for removal.

"The thing is," he said, when I mentioned weeding out the line, "I have a rule that nothing is to be taken out of it. I approved every single item before it was included and each one is there for a good reason. Even if sales are not high, eventually they'll all be reasonably well-selling articles."

I let that pass—for the moment—and we went on to Playboy Preferred, the direct mail merchandising effort.

"I've been wondering for some time," he told me, "whether we should offer merchandise for sale that in any way conflicts with advertisers in the magazine. With a massive investment like that to protect, it would be foolhardy to risk it for an in-and-out, quickie type of thing that might never have any repeat value."

We came to no firm decision; Hefner said he'd let the whole question simmer for awhile.

Then, somehow, we got onto Hefner's personal image with various groups—subscribers, college students, middle-class Americans and others.

"I don't think my identity varies with any of them," he insisted. "I think the mass media publicity I've been subjected to provides a picture that is universally accepted by everyone in the way I want it to be."

"And what's that?" I asked.

He sat swinging a slipper half off his foot, thought for a bit and then said, slowly, "As a man who has achieved everything he could possibly want, a man who enjoys every aspect of his life because every aspect is satisfying. I have a successful, thriving business and a beautiful home, lovely women are a part of my job, and I've got plenty of money to pursue my personal interests outside of business."

(A typical statement that Hefner has reiterated to the media in one form or another for years is: "I wouldn't trade places with anyone in the world. I have everything I've ever wanted—money, success in business, success in the arts. What I've done anybody else can do if he's willing to display a little of the initiative and derring-do that made the country great in the first place, instead of settling for job security, conformity, togetherness, anonymity, and slow death.")

"I think," he added, looking at me earnestly, "that this is the normal aspiration of most men, and that's why I think it is acceptable to everyone who comes in contact with me or my name."

"I don't know whether that's so," I said, "or whether, to the contrary, today's more sophisticated groups don't think you are an over-rich person guilty of over-kill in your fantasy of what you really want out of life."

"Doesn't your life style," I went on, getting wound up, "take on a fairly negligible significance when there are so many more pressing concerns constantly around us? Doesn't a wider range of people have a greater concern over racial equality in the U.S., for example, and over the U.S. not embarking on unqualified wars? Don't you and the way you live become infinitely less significant to these people than the pressures put upon them in their daily living, and the circumstances that worry them?"

"No, no," he said, "I don't believe that, I don't believe people are as concerned about what you feel they ought to be concerned about as they are about things closer to their own desires, like living the way Hugh Hefner lives."

(The decision to alter *Playboy's* policy against carrying articles on political and social problems resulted after Hefner was "whacked on the ass" by a policeman while he was watching a demonstration during the 1968 Democratic Convention in Chicago. As Lee Gottlieb, Playboy's public relations director, later summed up the incident: "That crystallized his [Hefner's] social consciousness." That whack may have changed one of the policies of the magazine but, as is obvious from this and other conversations with him, it didn't alter his self-image.)

"I'm sorry, I don't believe it," I told him, "I don't believe for one minute you are right, I think I am."

(Later, there was a conversation on the same theme during a meeting I attended with Hefner and several of his top executives. It was when the Big Bunny was being sent on its solo flight and I tried to point out to him that a $5.5 million plane was the wrong symbol for the identity that he ought to

25

be establishing for himself and the company in general.

("A majority of college students today will think your plane is so much bullshit and that you are bullshit and that you epitomize what's wrong with the country," I said.

(And, as he had before, he said, "No, I don't believe that."

(He was upset and he started puffing nervously on his pipe until he was almost hidden in a cloud of blue smoke. And he began to talk faster and to use his hands vigorously as he repeated, "I just don't believe that's so. In fact, I absolutely guarantee you that the majority of college students today are very much enamored with my life style and they would like it for themselves. I want you to take a poll of college students asking that specific question: 'What do you think of the Big Bunny and Hefner's use of it?' "

(He was dead serious about it but I told him I didn't think that could be included in the upcoming college student poll for the September 1970 issue, that perhaps it could be done later. Of course, it never was.)

Throughout all of the image discussion in the first interview, Hefner had a look on his face of "hey, you're disagreeing with me, wow, that's really something, you have moxie." And yet it was like play-acting, too. Not for me, I was making nothing more than a logical response to a rather narrow viewpoint, saying what almost any person would say. And yet this seemed to tickle him as though, gee, that's a great thing, this man's willing to challenge me, Hugh Hefner.

But I didn't feel anything of the sort. I thought what he was saying was wrong and told him why it was.

And yet, in thinking back over it, I say to myself, "My God, was everyone else really so submissive, really so acquiescent to everything he said that he wasn't even exposed to the slightest disagreement?"

But he lives in a womblike condition, there is probably no way that he doesn't live in a womblike condition. That occurred to me then and yet I thought, "Well, ok, if it makes him happy. I'm not here to make him unhappy but I'm not here just to make him happy, either."

All this time he was sucking noisily on his pipe. When

Hefner becomes engrossed in conversation, he starts fiddling with his pipe, lighting it and tamping it and taking out the tobacco and putting in fresh. So as we got deeper and deeper into the discussion, as he was becoming more challenged, he was sucking on the pipe more wildly every minute.

We talked for quite a while and finally he said, "I really must be going, I have to be at a party at the Ambassador." And he indicated his general pleasure with the session by saying, "Good show," as he walked out. The use of this expression is significant: It smacked of the 1950s. And why shouldn't it? Hefner is a 1950-ish person.

But my impression of him, at that meeting, was that here was a very quick, bright, perceptive individual whose glaring blind spot had to do with himself and his self-image. He struck me as being an extremely adept businessman, able to fit into a situation for which he did not have much background. He seemed to catch on a hell of a lot quicker than the Playboy people with whom I had dealt up to then.

Richard Rosenzweig, Hefner's executive assistant, intercepted me as I left and said, "You know, that really went over fantastically well."

"How do you know?" I asked.

"Oh," he said, "Hef would never have spent that much time with you if he wasn't enjoying it immensely." We had spent about two hours together.

"I enjoyed it, too," I said. "I think he's a very intelligent man."

"He's just so quick and bright," Rosenzweig replied, as any loyal executive assistant would have.

That ended the day.

As I left the mansion, I thought about Hefner and how he had changed over the years. Though it was impossible for me to realize what specific changes in character he 'had undergone, there was one thing I sensed for certain: The Hugh Hefner with whom I had met and conversed for several hours could never again be "keeper of the gate."

Chapter 2
Meeting The Gang

Two months before that talk with Hefner, when I was still executive vice president of a direct mail marketing firm called Whitney-Forbes, Inc., in Chicago, I began receiving letters and calls from an executive search firm. They're known in the trade as "headhunters" and this one was called Management Organization, Inc., the head of which was Allan J. Cox.

Most headhunters receive a fee that runs from 20 to 30 percent of the annual salary for the position they are trying to fill. Some rarely handle any position paying below $20,000 and still others will only stalk the $40,000 or more breed. About one thousand firms tagging themselves "executive search" are paid more than $35 million annually for their efforts. In 1958 there were only about a half-dozen such firms.

They're like a bunch of used car salesmen—a handful are reputable. Also, there is a fickleness about them: Making them aware of your general availability usually makes you a less attractive prospect.

In fact, Cox himself described his profession in a surprisingly frank manner in an article he wrote for *Playboy's* January 1972 issue, entitled "Confessions of a Corporate Head-Hunter." He said:

"I know the best way to impress management and I usually know if it's in a candidate's best interest to accept an offer. Superficially, these attainments make me an attractive person to know. Were it not for the fact that the profession I practice is probably the most opportunistic, cynical, defensive and manipulative of the corporate service industries, I would humbly agree with such an assessment."

At first I refused to see Cox—I had no reason to—but I finally agreed when he wrote that he wanted a recommendation from me for someone to fill a position for what he called a major client.

Cox is about 35. He has the classic salesman's handshake, the bone-crusher; he flashes a smile of at least 70 teeth, and he immediately goes to a first-name basis. Right off the bat he is very complimentary, tells you how much he's heard about you, what a super guy you must be, and how, just by shaking your hand, he can tell every word that he's heard is true.

Anyway, I asked him why he wanted a recommendation from me and he responded that everywhere he went, my name kept coming up. So I gave him some names and a background sketch of each man. After two hours of briefing he chose a name—mine. He offered me the job—mail order sales manager at Playboy Enterprises, Inc. I didn't have to think twice to reply:

"Do you think it's reasonable that someone sharing significantly in the profits of a corporation, and being its executive vice president, would leave it to join a company like Playboy in return for some meager salary?" He admitted it was hard to imagine.

I admit I was cocky. At 27, I had a vice presidency and an equity position in a company that was booming. And to go with the position there was money—a lot of it. My earnings that year were $246,000. Nevertheless, I decided to remain openminded, if only because I didn't want to be rude to Cox.

"Well," I said, "nothing is impossible and if the day should ever come that I decide to leave Whitney-Forbes, I will contact you before I do anything definite."

And that's exactly what I did a few months later when I left Whitney-Forbes.

The first thing Cox did was to set up a luncheon meeting with Robert S. Preuss, Playboy's business manager and associate publisher, considered the No. 2 man in the organization. Preuss brought the marketing director, Edward A. (Ted) Rogers, to the meeting with him.

I didn't think I was going to join Playboy under any circumstances so I discussed with them the ways they could improve their direct marketing activities. And I gave no indication of interest in joining Playboy myself. (I told Cox that I had heard rumblings in the business community that Playboy was mismanaged, disorganized and based too many of its business considerations on Hefner's whims. He didn't refute my comment, but it wasn't his job to do so.)

Cox called me after that luncheon and said, "Preuss was tremendously impressed but he feels that you have no deep interest in joining Playboy. Is this so? How can we make it worthwhile for you?"

"Tell them they're nice people, but really, I'm not meant for them and they're not meant for me. I have some hangups about the company and about the product they're selling and here, this will cinch it—tell them I wouldn't dream of going to work for them unless it were for at least a hundred thousand a year and probably more."

I picked that figure because I felt that it was far above what they were willing to pay for the position. After all, Cox had originally quoted only $40,000 a year. I thought to hell with it, that will get them off my back.

Surprisingly, Cox called the next day and said, "Preuss won't agree immediately to the $100,000 but he is willing to talk about it because he was so impressed by his conversation with you. He says they are not as messed up as you think they are, that you are basing your opinion on gossip and hearsay. Will you talk with him again?"

30

I met Preuss in his office for our second talk. As a director and executive vice president, his annual salary of $196,278 is second only to Hefner's $303,847. The 43-year-old Preuss is an accountant and was Hefner's college room-mate at the University of Illinois. He lives in what has been described as a "palatial, gadget-filled house" in the affluent west Chicago suburb of Hinsdale with his wife, Jean, and their three children.

He was warm and gracious, making me feel that he was really bending over backwards. Something else about him drew my attention. He was wearing a fluorescent green suit. He really was. It was a shiny deep green suit worn with a yellow shirt and a green, yellow and white tie and giant cufflinks. A conservative dresser, he wasn't.

And there was Preuss' office, too. I was somewhat impressed by it and yet in one way I was very "underwhelmed." Overall, the office gives you a feeling of tastefulness and opulence and quality of decor. The ceiling, for example, which is one of the most notable features, is concave over most of the room, with indirect lighting coming from it. It gives the effect of daylight when all the drapes are drawn.

There's a beautiful marble casement around the entire room and it's somewhat free-form-shaped. The walls curve in and out slightly, accenting the room's oval shape. The carpet is quite nice, white, in contrast to the dark brown of other offices in the building.

A color television and stereo unit are built into the wall. And also there is a refrigerator and wet-bar well stocked with Scotch, Preuss' favorite drink. All along the ledges around the office were piles of manila envelopes arranged in almost compulsively neat stacks, containing papers and correspondence.

Maybe it was as I got to know Preuss better that I started looking more closely. I saw that the office was a little on the seedy side; it looked as if things needed to be cleaned better than they usually were. There was somewhat of a pimp's apartment air about the place.

31

Preuss is the operational head of the company, after Hefner. Now, what that means is that he carries out all of Hefner's general dictums and a lot of his very nitty-gritty specific ones as well. He serves as the funnel to Hefner, disregarding Dick Rosenzweig. Preuss is really running the company under Hefner's direction and that he does superbly.

As much as anything, Preuss resembles a command post general who has a network of spies, of underlings who come to him for every decision that needs to be made and with every bit of information they can pass on. This is how, for example, when there is an interview, or a speech to be given, or when there is an overtime charge, Preuss is right on top of the situation.

It may be Anson Mount, in the public relations department, who will tell Preuss something the head of public relations, Lee Gottlieb, doesn't tell him. Or Nelson Futch, the promotion director, who passes on what the marketing director doesn't, or it may be John Mastro, the production director, who mentions something the editorial promotion staff hasn't.

But that day, as we began talking, I was really impressed by the fact that here was a man who was aware of a situation that had negatives in it, who knew that he had helped create it and who showed great enthusiasm for changing it.

This came up when he said he understood from Al Cox that I had some reservations about the firm. He wanted to know what they were and how I came to have such views. I decided to be brutally honest.

"I can't have my office a block from here," I explained, "and live across the street from Hefner and be a member of the business community without getting some general knowledge of Playboy. And I believe that Playboy's public image is a fairly direct manifestation of what it is.

"Now, believing that, this has to be one big Mickey Mouse organization, with a non-management philosophy that makes you a bunch of sycophants and yes-men."

He had no comeback and we began to discuss one of the key executives, whom I considered totally inept.

"He has his good points," Preuss asserted, "he's great at putting meetings together."

"That's the primary qualification for his position?" I asked.

"Well, he has other qualifications, too," Preuss informed me. "He's been in this business for a long time and he's written a book. He's been with two or three other publishers and a couple of agencies. He has really been around and he has a great reputation."

"I don't believe it," I said.

"You may be right or you may be wrong," Preuss replied, "but nevertheless, that's the point, that's why I want you to join this organization, so you can help change it."

When he said that, it hit me in the deepest way I can be hit—with the challenge of achieving a difficult objective. He set a variation on a theme that has really inspired me in so many of the things I have done and that is, meeting and beating the challenge of doing what I'm told can't be done.

So when Preuss said that I thought, "I'd like putting my mark on Playboy. I'd like for everyone to know me and say, 'He did more to change it than anybody else.' " I think in basic terms like that. It's important to me to know that I'm going to be able to make such an impression that for years they'll all say, "Remember Steve Byer? You couldn't forget him!"

With that gauntlet thrown at me, the idea of taking on Playboy and helping change it in a major way had a very strong appeal.

Preuss laid out a charter of my responsibilities and it had to do with sales and promotional efforts.

That included the promotion of key club membership sales; new and renewal magazine subscription sales; hotel room volume and the sales of Playboy products, the rabbit-identified merchandise sold through mail order advertising and in the clubs and hotels. It would involve Playboy Preferred Inc., the direct mail advertising subsidiary, and the Beneficial Standard Life Insurance program that was actually being run through Preferred. It might even involve such new

Playboy projects as the book club, record club, transportation service, all things that were then being considered.

And further, my area of influence would extend to the departments that in part provide the technical help for these efforts. For example, the computer performance area, to help make it a better service group to the mail marketing effort, and the purchasing department, and others that would be part of making other activities better and more productive. This was the realm of responsibility that Preuss and I were discussing. But my immediate concern was with Ted Rogers, because at that luncheon meeting he had demonstrated a total lack of assertiveness.

In the end I said to Preuss, "Look, one condition has to be that I'm not working for Ted Rogers." Rogers had only joined Playboy in March of 1969. In the previous three years he had been a corporate vice president of Metromedia, Inc., a big, highly diversified concern in the communications and entertainment fields. He served as director of corporate planning and assistant to the president at Metromedia. Preuss finally agreed that I would report to Rogers in name only.

Preuss and I then talked about some of the problems of the company. One, for example, concerned a core of people who at one time were fine in the capacity for which they had been hired but for whom the job had grown too big. Now they were in over their heads. If ever a company was plagued by the Peter Principle ("In a hierarchy every employee tends to rise to his level of incompetence"), it was Playboy.

Playboy's paramount problem was the fact that it lacked depth of management. This has been a chronic problem throughout its 18-year history. Preuss had realized this for years and said so in a 1968 interview with *Executive* magazine regarding Playboy's "enormous" potential: "It's probably limited only by the availability of people to do these things—staff is our biggest problem." At that time the company contended it was just beginning to build up middle management, noting that the top executives had been with Hefner since Playboy's early days. I could see no traces of middle management strength anywhere.

Even Hefner, as far back as 1961 when Playboy was just eight years old, pegged the problem. In an interview with some Harvard College academics, who were preparing a case study on Playboy, Hefner said: "I see a lot of employees with nothing to do, and others overburdened with work. Our management group is overworked. One of our big problems will be hiring capable people to come in and lighten the load."

So, why, with all of Playboy's vast financial resources, hadn't this major problem been solved? I could not answer that question, nor could Preuss. But as the conversation progressed, 1 began to get an inkling of what the answer might be.

"From what I've observed there are too many people in this organization who automatically bow to Hefner's wishes and whims," I said. Preuss nodded and said, "Yes, we must correct that. We must get people to think for themselves rather than to automatically assume that Hefner will or will not like something and that is the end-all."

"Perhaps that's why Playboy hasn't been able to attract assertive individuals," I suggested, adding, "In other words it could be the environment itself that lures and breeds the yes-man. Or maybe despite the stories that Hefner has been delegating more authority in recent years, his influence on the organization is just too pervasive."

Preuss did not comment on my conjectures. I could not tell whether he was reluctant to open a Pandora's box or if we had run out of time. In any case, the meeting ended a few minutes later with Preuss saying, "Look, I definitely feel that you are perfect for this job. Will you take it?"

"No, I won't. But I'll think further about it."

"All right, how much money do you want if you accept it?"

He knew the answer. I told him what I'd told Cox, "I'll do something like this for $100,000 a year and we'll see what happens after that."

Without hesitation, Preuss agreed. It didn't surprise me because I knew the company had sizable cash reserves, as well as tremendous potential for improvement. It did, however, tell me one thing—just how hungry Playboy was for young management talent. I still made no commitment.

The next day Rogers called to tell me that Preuss had filled him in on our meeting. Since I had promised to give serious thought to the offer, Rogers said, he wanted to set up a series of meetings with some of Playboy's other top executives, as well as Hefner himself.

"Why?" I asked him.

"So you can see how you'll get along with them and they with you," he explained.

I agreed. Several days later I met with each of them. All I knew about them was what Ted Rogers had told me, which I had to take with several pounds of salt.

My first meeting was with the personnel director, Theo Frederick, a 40-ish bleached blond, a fairly attractive woman, who was the third wife of Playboy's renowned editorial director, the late A.C. (Auguste Comte) Spectorsky. They were married in 1955. She has two sons from her prior marriage, one of whom is Brooke, a TV director in Cleveland; the other, Lance, until recently worked for Playboy in Chicago. Theo and "Spec" lived quite comfortably in their north Michigan Avenue apartment near the Playboy Building.

Theo was a stencil clerk until Spectorsky spotted her among the clutter of stencil clerks and decided to marry her, at which point she became personnel director. She prides herself on being a very with-it woman but she doesn't carry it off successfully. And I remember being amused when she went into a routine of "yeah, man," and other such conversational gambits that were meant to say, "Look, I can rap with you."

Theo also likes to strike a note of confidentiality between herself and the person she's talking to so she said, "Look, man, I know your background. I'm aware that you are known in your business as being a real tough nut, a hard apple, a cutthroat who will do anything that is necessary in order to achieve whatever it is you wish to achieve. Now, if that can just be tempered here, that's what we need."

36

People frequently say exactly the opposite of what they mean. This struck me about Theo in her statement that I could really do great things for the company if I could just somehow funnel this rough and tumble nature into a totally positive direction. So Theo and I rapped for a couple of hours.

Next was Arnold Morton. Morton, 49, who is a senior vice president and director of the club-hotel division, which was called Playboy Clubs International (PCI) until late in 1971. He makes $103,278 a year, which affords him a comfortable life with his second wife, Zorine, a former Gaslight girl, and their four children in suburban Highland Park, on Chicago's north shore.

When PCI was formed in 1959, a portion of its stock was owned by Hefner, Morton and Victor A. Lownes, currently vice president of Playboy's international division. As of January 1971, Playboy owned nearly 70 percent of PCI's stock, Hefner owned 20.6 percent and Morton 9.8 percent. Lownes had sold his PCI stock back to the company prior to that year. During January and February of 1971 the company acquired all the PCI shares held by Hefner and Morton through an exchange of the company's common stock for the PCI stock. Hefner received 195,373 shares worth more than $4.5 million; Morton's 92,921 were worth about $2.1 million. These estimates are based upon the market value of $23.50 a share that Playboy common stock was selling at through its initial public offering in November of 1971.

Morton comes from a long line of restaurant people. His parents own Morton's Restaurant on Chicago's South Shore Drive and Arnie worked for them when he was young. Then he opened a bar on Rush Street called the Walton Walk. He started with Hefner as head of the Chicago Playboy Club in 1960. The economy was good then and consequently, the Playboy Club prospered. And so did Arnie.

Well, Arnie is basically a fine man, loyal and pretty hard-working. He is blunt and kind of rough around the edges compared to, say, the suave, sophisticated Spectorsky, who

37

was his counterpart in the editorial domain of the Playboy empire. Morton doesn't care about editorial, his bailiwick is the clubs and that's all that is important to him. Spectorsky was downright apathetic to the clubs and hotels and to what they're all about. It is as if both men were working for different companies in totally unrelated fields.

(This dichotomy of feelings is another example that helps shatter the long-standing myth regarding the camaraderie within the Playboy organization. I discuss it more fully in a subsequent chapter, "All In The Family." At the time of these meetings, however, I had no particular insight into the camaraderie situation at Playboy.)

Arnold and I sat in his office, which like Preuss' had some nice touches to it. The walls were paneled, with a large TV screen built into the wall and a built-in set of digital clocks showing the various time zones around the world. Arnold really never has time to watch television, but God forbid somebody should try to take it out—he'd have a stroke. Anyway, if there had been a huge world map dotted with pin flags hanging on the other wall, it might have been the office of some high-ranking general.

Shortly after we began talking I realized Arnold's feelings about the magazine division. He said the magazine was good for only one thing and that was to attract new keyholders and to sell merchandise. That was his prerogative, of course. And as far as my pending role in the company was concerned, again Arnold thought only in terms of the clubs. Would my efforts sell more keys and more merchandise?

One area I gingerly avoided in the course of our conversation was the trouble Playboy had gotten into, years earlier, when it was trying to get its New York City Playboy Club off the ground. Morton admitted paying a $50,000 bribe to the New York State Liquor Authority's chairman in 1961 to get a license. Because of the politically corrupt situation that existed then, Morton said at the time, the bribe had to be paid. It was carried on Playboy's books as "legal, promotional, travel and entertainment expenses," by Playboy's then chief bookkeeper, Preuss. The incident blew over pretty smoothly and Playboy has had no similar ones like it since.

Arnold and I chatted for about an hour and a half. As I left he said, "You're ok, why don't you come here and straighten out some of these people?" Arnold is a lot of bluster, a lot of talk and nowhere near that much action or follow-through on what he's going to do to someone if he doesn't shape up. At least, when I walked out of his office it was with the feeling that Arnold had been honest with me.

The next session was with Spectorsky, who had been Playboy's associate publisher and editorial director for 16 years. Born 61 years ago in Paris of American parents, Auguste Comte Spectorsky was named for the 19th Century French Positivist philosopher who added the word "sociology" to the language. He died of a stroke last January while he and Theo were vacationing in the Virgin Islands. Of all the Playboy top brass, "Spec" was the most professionally prominent. He had been hired by Hefner from the National Broadcasting Company in 1956, three years after *Playboy* was founded, for the primary purpose of upgrading the magazine's fiction and to make it a more sophisticated package in general. (Sophistication has always been a favorite word around Playboy.)

At that time he had already made a name for himself in literary circles as the author of *The Exurbanites*, a bestseller about New York City's commuters that has since become a sociological classic. With his intellectual air and New York savvy, Spectorsky projected a suave, scholarly image, belying the magazine's image then. In 1956 a good deal of the fiction in *Playboy* still consisted of reprints of long-forgotten works by such authors as John Steinbeck, Erskine Caldwell, Somerset Maugham, Robert Ruark, Ray Bradbury. Most name writers shunned writing for *Playboy*. Those that didn't contributed their second-rate works. But all of this changed, due in good part to the efforts of Spectorsky.

I was anxious to meet Spectorsky. After all, who in the organization, other than Hefner, would know more about the magazine, and know its future direction better, than the man who had been second in command of it for all those years? And considering his editorial acumen and intellectual reputation, who else was there who could be as objective and articulate? Unfortunately, the "who" wasn't Spectorsky, at least at first.

My meeting with "Spec" began by being the least professionally illuminating about Playboy, and yet perhaps the most illuminating about the person. Spectorsky started by merely paying lip service to why we were meeting.

"Well, I guess we're here because you're considering joining the company," he said. "Is there anything you would like to hear from me that I can or should say to you?"

"Only what you want to," I told him, wondering if by chance I was meeting with the wrong A.C. Spectorsky.

"We have our problems and I suppose we're sort of messed up in a few ways, but Hef's a great man, a wonderful man. I owe him everything. Is there anything else I can tell you?"

I still couldn't believe that the man sitting before me was A.C. Spectorsky, editorial director of one of the most successful magazines in publishing history, whose annual salary of $182,606 made him one of the highest-paid individuals in his profession. Was he being condescending? Or was he merely curt by nature? In any case, I refused to panic.

"I'm sort of curious," I mused. "You're editorial director and associate publisher of *Playboy,* you've been here for fifteen years and I'm surprised you don't have anything more to say."

My comment apparently made sense because Spectorsky, after a slight pause, said, "I just didn't think you'd be interested."

"Why do you think I'm here?" I asked. "I hear nothing but bullshit about this company. I'm here because I'm trying to learn something more about you, your staff, the company, how it's made up, what's wrong with it, what's right with it . . ."

And he looked at me and said, "Well, you know, I'm used to dealing with idiots who don't ask questions like that."

"I guess, then," I said, "I have a major problem. Could you

manage to deal with me differently because I'm not such an idiot?"

And he pondered this and said, "I don't know, I don't know."

After that it was an interesting conversation because he did open up, but throughout the meeting we were both aware that it had started off in an uncomfortable manner.

Spectorsky outlined the nature of his activities, the editorial involvement, and where the problem areas were. About an hour later there was no doubt in my mind that the gentleman I was conversing with was A.C. Spectorsky, associate publisher and editorial director of *Playboy* magazine.

One key executive was conspicuously missing, though not intentionally. He was Victor A. Lownes III, who as head of Playboy's international division lives and works in London. He travels to the U.S. about twice a year.

I had met Lownes in 1960 when I met Hefner. A University of Chicago Business School graduate, Lownes has been with Playboy almost from the beginning. As promotion director for many years, he was responsible for numerous stunts that helped put Playboy in the public eye. One of his major contributions is the design of the Playboy Bunny costume. He is intelligent, has a creative flair and, where I was concerned, a short temper, as I was to discover.

At 43, Lownes is as flamboyant as ever. He calls himself "extravagant and pompous," and he proves it in his life style. He lives hard, fast and expensively. He is divorced. Like Preuss, Morton and Spectorsky, Lownes became a millionaire from his stock holdings in Playboy. A few years ago he sold about $1.8 million worth back to the company because, as he explained, "I wanted a couple of million to play with." He still had more than $2 million worth of stock left.

(Playboy executives, for some reason, always seem to need large sums of money. Spectorsky, for example, received an annual salary of $182,606, with an additional $16,904 contributed to a profit-sharing plan. Yet, during 1970 and 1971 he borrowed $134,400 from a Chicago bank, pledging as collateral 19,600 shares of Playboy common stock. Then in March 1971 he borrowed $140,000 more from Playboy's profit-sharing plan. I don't know what he used the money for, although "Spec" did sport a big yacht and owned a home in St. Croix in the Virgin Islands. But he was still nowhere the high liver that, say, Lownes is.)

Lownes makes $75,639 a year, hardly enough to sustain his passion for sports cars. He has owned several, including the $50,000 Aston-Martin DB-5 used in the James Bond movies. If it's good enough for 007, it's good enough for Lownes.

Nothing about Lownes is subdued. Even his clothes tell the story. When I finally did see Victor some months later, he was wearing a plaid suit with a matching plaid tie and shirt. His constant companion was Connie Kreski, the 1969 Playmate of the Year.

A Chicago newspaper once observed that Lownes' "personal life has gone public several times." In 1962 he was sued for assault in a brawl in a Chicago nightclub. The suit was dismissed. Two years later, a former Playboy Bunny won a paternity suit against him. He appealed the suit, lost and finally settled out of court. Then in 1967 he was beaten and robbed of $80 by four youths in Chicago's Old Town area.

I am not sure why Lownes was banished to London, but somewhere along the line, he probably irritated Hefner. Or perhaps his overt bid to become Playboy of the Western World was tarnishing the image Playboy executives have been striving to convey for so long, that of being sophisticated businessmen.

Nevertheless, Lownes remains steadfast to Hefner and Playboy if for no other reason than a therapeutic one. He admitted it last March when he told *Forbes*: "I'm here for my psyche, not money. Playboy is my identity."

It could just as well have been Hefner talking.

Chapter 3
On The Road To Playboy

A long, black Mercedes limousine stood in lonely dignity in the driveway. Two faceless bodyguards wearing black overcoats flanked the grillwork gate that led past the neatly manicured lawn into a cloistered vestibule, monitored by a closed-circuit television camera. Next to the black grillwork front door a lone button protruded. I pushed it and spoke into the voice box. "I'm Stephen Byer. I have an appointment with Mr. Rosenzweig."

The Playboy Mansion greets a visitor with a somewhat cold, sophisticated air . . . the high black iron-grilled fence . . . the red brick facade . . . the meticulously kept lawn . . . the soft-spoken black doorman who leads you to the anteroom. It's the palace of a recluse, the gates locking in, not keeping out. The immediate feeling of security gobbles you up. Time stands still. There are no night nor day nor even seasons. You have entered Hugh Marston Hefner's world—his personally created environment—where he has worked, eaten, slept and played for a good part of the past thirteen years.

Hefner's 54-room edifice, located at 1340 N. State Parkway on Chicago's Near North Side, is valued at nearly $1 million. It is down the street from the swank Ambassador Hotel on a high-rent block mixed with stately refurbished brownstones and high rises. The Mansion is owned by Playboy and leased to Hefner at a modest $650 a month, probably the cheapest rent in the city for similar accommodations. It was formerly the home of a wealthy physician who reportedly had entertained Chicago's blue bloods and other notable guests such as Teddy Roosevelt.

Playboy recently acquired an adjoining 20-room structure as an annex to the Mansion, along with another 29-room mansion in a Los Angeles suburb, at an aggregate cost of $1.6 million. Playboy says it uses the mansions for "charitable functions and a wide variety of promotional activities by corporate officers."

I was at the Mansion to meet Hefner. Before that, however, I had to talk with Richard Rosenzweig, Hefner's trusty assistant who for the past eleven years has acted as a clearing house for all matters requiring his master's personal attention. Rosenzweig, 35, is the only Playboy executive who works out of the Mansion. He screens most of Hefner's calls and sits in on all his meetings other than those dealing with editorial matters.

Dick is a meticulously mod dresser whose attire is always in vogue. He, too, likes the good life but lives it in a much more orderly way than, say, Lownes. While Dick drives a Mercedes 250 SE convertible, he is still not too proud to ride a bicycle on any Sunday afternoon from his apartment near the Mansion to nearby Lincoln Park or to various art galleries around town. He favors himself as a connoisseur of art and the curator for Hefner's rather impressive art collection. Dick was divorced but has recently remarried.

Rosenzweig, a Northwestern University graduate, had been a business reporter for Dun & Bradstreet before joining Playboy in 1958 as an advertising salesman. Not long after, the word went out that Hefner needed an assistant. Dick applied, got the job and has had it ever since. From what I gathered he wouldn't trade it for any other position.

Dick has a pleasing smile, a warm personality and tact when it comes to handling people. He is viewed generally as a Playboy executive (his title is vice president), but among most of the top executives of the company there was always the qualification in each of our minds that he was only the voice to and from Hefner. As Hefner's emissary, showing people around the Mansion falls to him. It is a job he obviously relishes and one would think that it's his house he is flaunting to visitors.

I waited for a couple of minutes to be greeted by the firm handshake and broad, toothy smile of Dick Rosenzweig. I thought he was going to take me to see Hefner immediately, but he didn't. Instead, he offered a tour of the Mansion. This courtesy somehow gave me the feeling that such a tour was requisite to meeting Hefner. So I submitted.

The Mansion's interior emphasizes the formality of upper-class living; fine and expensive living. The silence is funereal, the red tweedy carpeting absorbs noise, the walls are festooned with Picasso, DeKooning, Kline, Gallo, Klee, Pollock—art that's original, contemporary and costly. (I would estimate the art in the Mansion and that at the Playboy offices is worth at least two-and-a-half-million dollars.)

The initial feeling is that this is not the cozy, intimate pad of some with-it swinger. But as you begin entering specific rooms that feeling suddenly changes. There is the sprawling wood-paneled living room or so-called Great Hall, whose walls are adorned with contemporary paintings. A counter-high electronics unit with speakers reaching into every corner bisects the room. A game table, basking in lights that swing out on cranes at the touch of a button, stands in the middle of the room. Two repairmen are on duty around the clock to make sure everything works to perfection. And it does.

Soon it seems that there is little or nothing to do in the place but play games. Downstairs is a game room with a variety of pinball machines surrounding a pool table. There are other rooms with ping pong tables and a sauna, of course. The bar also is downstairs and for the more active guests can be reached by sliding down a brass firehouse pole. It has a window that provides an underwater view of the kidney-shaped swimming pool set in tropical decor. If guests really want seclusion, they may swim underwater for a very short distance and surface into a room furnished with soft cushions and background music. I never made it to that one.

The top floor of the Mansion is used as a dormitory for about 30 Bunnies who work at the Chicago Playboy Club. It, naturally, is very much off-limits. During the warmer months the Mansion roof becomes a sun deck for the Bunnies, who often do their sunning in the nude. (Just ask the tenants who live in the surrounding high rises.)

Hefner's duplex consists of a living room, bedroom and a small adjoining room used as a TV taping studio. It is all ankle-deep in white carpet and you only walk on it with shoes off. On Hefner's bathroom wall, hanging in a frame, is one share of *Esquire* stock as a reminder of the time he worked for *Esquire,* not long before he started *Playboy.* Under the framed certificate is a sign that instructs: "In case of emergency, break glass."

Overnight guests of Hefner's are sometimes given the Gold Room, which contains a billowy waterbed for those who like a lot of wave action.

Throughout the tour Rosenzweig and I chatted mainly about the art in the Mansion. He almost seemed disinterested in me as a prospective Playboy executive and what I could offer the company. He was trying to establish a rapport on the basis of our common interest in art, rather than on what our mutual thoughts on Playboy and business were. But it really made little difference to me at that point. Perhaps I was just tired of greeting and meeting Playboy executives. It was the Master of the House I was anxious to meet.

The tour ended after an hour or so and Rosenzweig led me to the conference room, assuring me that Hefner would be there shortly . . .

After that talk with Hefner, I left the Mansion for my apartment, about a half-block away. The walk hardly gave me a chance to gather my thoughts, but by the time the elevator reached the fifth floor, there were two aspects of my situation that began to tug at me. One was a moral consideration, the other entirely business.

How, I wondered, could I give my loyalty to a company that based its conceptualization, product and services upon one of the most glaring weaknesses of human nature—sexual fantasy. That was the reason I hadn't read *Playboy* or frequented a Playboy Club since 1960. The Playmate in the magazine's centerfold and the Bunny in the club provide only the most vicarious and imaginary substitutes for a real life sex partner. Take, for example, the Bunnies. Every characteristic of the costume, every mannerism, every word they are instructed to say, is centered around this surrogate sex partner concept. Playboy does not recognize a truly human relationship.

So I had a long-standing, deep-seated bias against Playboy, viewing the company as one of the most negative and immoral of any in the U.S. My meetings with Hefner and the rest of the Playboy brass had somewhat softened my prejudices, but had failed to dispel them.

Holding those views, how could I justify joining Playboy? To do so, I put the question out of my mind because there was no way I could successfully counter it against my stronger desires for the money, power and prestige Playboy had to offer. I also did some fast and furious rationalizing concerning the vague prospect that maybe someday things would change at Playboy; that perhaps I could be instrumental in bringing change about. I suppose man can come up with reasons for anything, be it God or war. Consequently, I dismissed my moral consideration by pretending it didn't exist.

But there was still the business consideration nagging me. Somehow big business and I never hit it off right. I had had my fill of corporate bureaucracy, the politicking and intrigue, the backstabbing, the pettiness. It left an acid taste in my mouth. But I still believed in that sound business principle: As long as I was learning about business it was better to make mistakes with other people's money than with my own. With this thought, I began to reflect upon the first ten years of my business career. And there was plenty to reflect upon.

As previously mentioned, my first real job was with Fuller & Smith & Ross, the Chicago ad agency. The job was not without its pressures. While I liked the excitement of advertising, my stomach didn't. At eighteen, I had the ulcers to prove it. The ulcers convinced me that I had to quit advertising and they also convinced the Army that I would be one soldier who in no way could travel on his belly.

About two weeks after I quit the agency, I landed a job as salesman in a respectable art gallery, earning a respectable $150 a week. The pace was therapeutic. I learned to accept problem situations more calmly and to recognize the need for flexibility in business. For the next eight months I sold paintings, created local ads and designed exhibition programs. My ulcers healed. So I left the gallery to resume my studies at the University of Illinois at Champaign. (That was when I met Barbara Sokolec, a Chicago girl attending the university, who later became my wife.)

But my yen for the business world was too strong—I became a part-time student and took a full-time job with a small ad agency called Richard Newman Associates. In the eighteen months that I was responsible for bringing in new business, the agency's billings boomed from $200,000 to $1,200,000. I felt my efforts were worth more than the $80 a week I was earning. Unfortunately, the head of the agency didn't offer me more and I still had a business naivete that made me shy about asking for a raise. So I left for a greener field—$20 a week greener.

The *Daily Illini*—the University of Illinois newspaper— became my new employer. Selling ad space and coordinating production activities added still another dimension to my business savvy. Six months later the lure of big business was dangled in front of me.

Based upon the results of a successful subscription ad campaign I had handled at the *Illini* for Cowles Communications, Inc., publisher of *Look* magazine, I was offered a job as a direct mail copywriter for *Look*. It was like getting called up from the minor to the major leagues. Although I must admit the thought of living in Des Moines, Iowa, Cowles home base, didn't exactly excite me. It certainly was no Chicago. But then, neither was Champaign. I joined Cowles in June 1963. Barbara and I were married the following summer.

The job paid $8,000 a year, with a guaranteed review six months later that might get me up to $8,500. The staff consisted of fourteen copywriters plus two copy chiefs.

After three months at Cowles, I had made two major discoveries. The first, I hated copywriting with a purple passion. The second, there appeared to be an obvious flaw in Cowles' overall operation.

This huge facility, occupying two square blocks and employing almost three thousand people, was being used solely for the circulation, promotion and fulfillment of *Look*. The work force was fully utilized only during the peak seasons, in early fall and immediately before Christmas. But this glut of personnel was kept the entire year because Cowles had established itself as the father-figure of Des Moines. You didn't have to be a management consultant to see the inefficiency and waste of the situation.

At that time Cowles was performing subscription fulfillment services as a favor for a Cincinnati-based publication called *Farm Quarterly*. The cost was a nominal $16,000 a year. As a diversion from my copywriting chores, I had wangled the job of writing renewal schedules for *Farm Quarterly*. It was, of course, a tedious function, but it gave me the opportunity to attract the attention of Lester Suhler, a Cowles vice president and director of subscription sales, who also happened to be my boss.

I persuaded Suhler that improvement was needed in *Farm Quarterly's* promotional materials and that a trip to Cincinnati to discuss the changes was essential.

The response of *Farm Quarterly* executives was enlightening, so much so that I decided to return to Des Moines via New York City—without consulting Suhler. If we were able to perform promotion and fulfillment services for *Farm Quarterly,* we could do it for other publishers as well, I reasoned. I started searching for potential prospects.

I picked three publishers I thought were established enough to be profitable, yet not so large as to have fulfillment facilities of their own. They were Universal Publishing, which published *Golf, Ski* and *Family Handyman; National Review*, William F. Buckley Jr.'s publication, and *Saturday Review*. Universal and *National Review* agreed to turn over their fulfillment efforts to Cowles. Though the *Saturday Review* was satisfied with its own fulfillment service, I was able to sell it on Cowles doing a subscription promotion package. Incidentally, that promotional package they paid $750 for seven years ago is still being used.

Upon returning to Cowles, I happily informed Suhler that we now had four accounts. "What are you talking about, scout?" he asked with a trace of skepticism in his voice. I gave him a full narrative of the preceding week. We discussed it and Suhler said, "I think it's a fine idea, let's figure out how much it will cost and charge a little bit more and we'll take them on." And we did.

In about a year and a half, the number of accounts had spurted—from four to sixty-five—and so had my salary. During this period my pay doubled to $16,000 a year. In the meantime, what I had created now amounted to a little division, informal and with no budget, but with a big dollar potential.

In addition, as my contacts around the country grew, I began getting fairly attractive job offers. One in particular was to result in my learning about a side of corporate life of which I was totally ignorant.

The job offer I refer to was made by Malcolm Smith, head of RTV Sales, a New York-based mail-order operation. Besides a higher base salary than I was making, I would also get one-half of one percent of RTV's profits. Based on the previous year's results, that amounted to $10,000. That was the kind of incentive that made sense.

Torn between this generous offer and a job I liked doing, I confronted Suhler with my dilemma over lunch one day. His reaction was both flattering and surprising. After I outlined

50

the offer, Suhler thought for a few moments and said: "Tell you what, let's make a deal." He began scratching figures on a napkin and minutes later the Suhler plan lay before me.

It said first 200P (meaning $200,000 in profits)—base 20 (or $20,000 in base pay); next 200P—$5,000 bonus; next 100P—$5,000 bonus, and then the balance on a sliding scale of bonuses so that with increased profits I kept getting a higher percentage up to a ceiling of 8 percent of the pre-tax profits.

This meant that the division would have to show a $200,000 profit before I earned my base salary. It also meant I must increase my efforts considerably, since profits the previous year had amounted to $100,000. I told Suhler I'd think about it.

The next day we met again, bandying about various figures and percentages. The result was a slight increase for the second hundred thousand profit but the ceiling was still pegged at 8 percent. I was satisfied. We sealed the negotiations with a firm handshake. It was my first big business deal and I didn't know that the only safe seal is a name signed on a contract. Even if I had, I wouldn't have thought of asking Suhler for one. I felt our relationship was too close to question his honor. I was as sure of his as I was of my own.

Suhler and I made our agreement in March of 1965 but it wasn't until about six months later that business moved into high gear. So the big profits didn't start to appear until 1966. I watched every penny to keep costs low. I wouldn't even allow the offices to be painted because of the $800 overhead charge. The profits were rolling in.

When the audited 1966 figures reached my desk, a warm and very secure feeling came over me. I had more than made my base of $20,000: Cowles owed me about $108,000. The division had earned profits of nearly two and a half million dollars.

I asked Suhler when the bonus would be paid and he answered, "Well, pretty soon, scout, we're going to get that money to you." But while I was gloating in Suhler's office over a bill for $108,000, the top Cowles executives were sitting around in New York saying, "What do we do about this guy? How do we take care of this situation?"

Their first course of action was to evade me. Suddenly the people I had been in close contact with—Suhler; Gardner "Mike" Cowles, chairman; Marvin C. Whatmore, president— were not around or were unavailable whenever I called.

So, after three months of playing hide-and-seek, I walked into Whatmore's New York office unannounced, with the year-end tally sheet and profit statement tucked under my arm. "Marvin," I said, "I'm terribly concerned and I'd like to straighten something out. Cowles owes me $108,000 and here's why." I showed him the figures and the Suhler-Byer deal spelled out on the napkin. He was silent but I persisted: "I think you know the money is owed to me, so where's my check?"

"Oh, yes, Steve," he said, "Suhler and I have been meaning to discuss this with you." And he told his secretary to call Suhler to his office. Suhler arrived in about five minutes and nodded hello—not a word, though—and Whatmore said, "Les, you have that memo from Merrill Clough (controller)?"

"No, Marvin, I haven't," Les said, so Marvin sent for the memo on Byer and the contracts division.

It was dated a month earlier and was from Clough to Karl Haase, assistant secretary of the company, with carbons to Whatmore and Suhler. It said, "It has been determined that the contract services group has been a serious drain on the overhead of the Des Moines facility. Therefore, we are adjusting the overhead burden to its rightful position from the previously recommended 18 percent of direct salaries to 72 percent of direct salaries, retroactive to January 1, 1965, and all records are to be adjusted to reflect this proper level."

I read it and went into a rage. I could barely contain myself. I almost took hold of the edge of his desk and turned it over on him. My hand was shaking, the paper was crinkling and there was dead silence in the room. Whatmore wasn't saying a word, nor was Suhler.

The words were swimming before my eyes and the sentences weren't making sense but I knew what they said.

52

Finally I steadied myself and said, "I haven't figured it out yet, except very broadly, but I think that the alteration in overhead burden reduces the pre-tax profit of my operation to $200,000 or slightly below."

"I don't know about that," Whatmore said, "I haven't figured it out. Whatever it comes to, it comes to, and I think we'd better get the accountants to work on it."

I said something nasty and he said, "Now look here, there's no need for that kind of foul talk in here, this is simply an accounting matter, I didn't have anything to do with it."

That's when I said "bullshit" and flicked the paper on his desk and walked out, went to my hotel, packed and flew to Des Moines.

I was in my office the next day when Suhler walked in and said, "How're you doing, scout?"

"What difference does it make?" I snapped.

"I don't want you to be upset by these accounting adjustments," he told me.

I stood up, closed my door and asked Suhler to sit down. I stood over him and said, "I understand why you did this. It was because there are directors of this company earning vastly less than I did. I also realize that when you set up the deal on that napkin, you never anticipated I would earn the kind of profit I did. You thought you'd never have to pay me more than $20,000 a year. I know that the accounting adjustment was the only solution Clough could come up with to get me back down to $20,000 a year when I should have gotten $128,000."

He didn't say a word or make a sound.

"I'll tell you one other thing, Les," I went on, "I want a check for $15,000 by tomorrow afternoon, simply as blood money, because Cowles owes me a lot more than that. If I get it, I'll stay for a reasonable period of time. If I don't, I'll quit."

I turned away, walked to my desk, sat down and swiveled around, facing out the window. I couldn't look at him because I was crying. I was that upset that Suhler had let this thing be done to me. He left without saying a word.

The following afternoon, an envelope containing a check for $15,000 was delivered to me. But from then on my heart wasn't in the job.

I cashed the check and immediately began looking for a job. About ten months later I left Cowles to join Whitney-Forbes, Inc., a Chicago-based direct mail merchandising company, owned by my wife's uncle, Albert E. Sloan. I was familiar with the Whitney-Forbes operation because it had been one of my major accounts at Cowles, representing a quarter of a million dollars in profit. Both Barbara and I were happy to be returning to Chicago with our son, Matthew, who was then one year old.

My agreement with Sloan was that I would secure business in return for a percentage of the net pre-tax profits on the various programs other than the accounts Whitney-Forbes already had. I also had been especially careful in establishing the ground rules as to how overhead was to be allocated. Overhead was allocated in direct proportion to the sales volume of his accounts versus mine. This time I made sure I had a contract in order to avoid another Cowles fiasco.

Whitney-Forbes was located in the Merchandise Mart with a staff of only two, Sloan, who was then 63, and his secretary. My title was executive vice president and I set out to earn it on the Monday following Thanksgiving Day of 1967.

Within eighteen months I had brought in a number of accounts. They included such companies as Citgo, Sunray DX, Sunoco, Imperial Oil Ltd. of Canada, Bond Stores, Shell, Arco (then Atlantic Richfield), Universal Publishing, United Equitable Life Insurance Co., Bank Americard and Mobil. Most of these companies represented more than one program.

Business was booming. We had moved from our 400-square-foot space at the Merchandise Mart to the prestigious John Hancock Center, occupying 3,000 square feet. Our three-man operation had expanded to include an administrative coordinator, a creative director, a production manager, a controller, additional clerical and secretarial help and a bookkeeper. With gross sales running into the millions, we were no longer a small company. We would soon be big league.

And as for my earnings, the first six months I drew around $30,000 against my percentage interest. In the following twelve months I earned $246,000, my highest year's earnings.

My pace at Whitney-Forbes was quite a hectic one. In the course of a week I'd be running off to New York, Toronto and Tulsa. I was spending more time on the road and less time in the office. Communication between Sloan and myself began to wane. And neither of us realized the significance of the situation until it was too late.

It was shortly after I had sold two particular programs that the communications gap caught up with both of us. Elated over the relative ease of the sale, I went to Sloan's office on a Friday morning to share the good news.

"Al," I said, "the most amazing thing has happened and I have to tell you. I just made the two easiest sales of my life. Two clients just bought our new watch offer."

Sloan's response wasn't as enthusiastic as I had anticipated. He merely acknowledged the sale, giving me the feeling that I had not heard the last of it.

The following Monday I was doing some paper work when Sloan came in and asked me to see him in his office. I said sure and grabbed a cup of coffee, went to his office and asked what was up . . .

The conversation resulted in a clashing of egos and a dispute over accounts. The differences were irreconcilable, leading to my resignation about ten days later.

This time there had been no tears nor fiery speeches, just a final goodbye and cash settlement—a check for $108,000.

Chapter 4
The Making of A Veep

The sweat running down the sides of my face felt good. For the first time in days, I wasn't wearing a suit and tie, just dirty blue jeans and a faded sweat shirt. Barbara, with her hair pinned up and also garbed in jeans and an old shirt, looked just as messy. We were hanging paintings in our newly decorated apartment. I had decided to table any thoughts about Playboy, hoping to gain a new perspective after a day or so. It was going to be a long weekend of loafing—not pondering, reflecting or analyzing—just loafing.

Thoughts about Playboy, Cowles, Whitney-Forbes, my future, were the farthest things from my mind when the buzzer rang. "A messenger from Playboy to see you, Mr. Byer," the doorman announced.

"Please send him up," I said.

Both Barbara and I were in for a surprise. It wasn't a "him." It was a luscious-looking, a delectable-looking young girl, who introduced herself as "Bridget from personnel." She was dressed in a green wool mini and had beautiful legs, radiant auburn hair and a deep tan—a good-looking chick.

Neither Barbara nor I said a word, Bridget did the talking. "Miss Frederick asked me to deliver this to you," she said, handing me an envelope.

I thanked her and rang for the elevator. All the time she was fluttering her eyelashes and smiling as if she were doing a toothpaste commercial. (Beautiful Bridget, what a blow it was when I discovered, about a week later, that her last name was—Horowitz!)

The envelope Bridget had delivered contained a complimentary Playboy Club membership card with a note from Theo Frederick saying, "I hope this will be the final straw bringing you over to joining us. We really hope you will." It, of course, wasn't the final straw. However, that evening I told Barbara I had reached a decision. I would join Playboy . . .

The next day I phoned Preuss to accept the job. We met that afternoon and he welcomed me into the Playboy organization with a handshake. It was a Thursday and I told him that I wanted to begin on Monday. There were no second thoughts about my decision over the weekend. In fact, I tried not to think about Playboy. It was the first time in weeks my mind was uncluttered with names, faces, dates and such. The time was for Barbara and Matthew, who was now three years old, and our second son, four-month-old Josh.

Maybe the seeds of my leaving Playboy were sowed in the first hour of that first day, when I won a running battle with the personnel department over "reporting" there. Before I had a chance to sit down my temporary secretary, Barbara Rosenthal, greeted me in one breath and in the next she relayed a blunt, arrogant message: "You are to report to personnel with no delay. It is routine procedure for every new employee to check in there first."

Suddenly I felt my old foe—corporate bureaucracy—creeping up on me. The thought was unnerving. "Absolutely not," I shouted, "tell them if they have something for me to sign to send it up and I'll sign it. Otherwise, I don't need a manual telling me how Playboy began. Don't bother me with it again." Suddenly, I was reminded of ulcers.

That didn't end it because, as I learned later, Theo Frederick's secretary took it upon herself to show me that I was no different than any other new employee. If she had the authority to make others go through this little indoctrination, she had the authority to order me to do so.

Consequently, she called and said, "You just tell Mr. Byer that he is required to check in with the personnel department. We'll expect him here immediately."

"You call that bitch back and tell her to go fuck herself," I thundered, biting my lip to keep from laughing. Without hesitation or a blush, Barbara calmly picked up the phone, called Theo's secretary and in a most cordial and soft-spoken tone said: "Mr. Byer has instructed me to call you and to tell you to go fuck yourself." Now that's what I call an unflappable secretary. (She eventually became my permanent secretary.) Anyway, that ploy apparently had just the right finesse because I didn't receive any more phone calls from personnel nor was I ever indoctrinated.

Then there was the matter of my title. In midafternoon Ted Rogers called to welcome me to the company. "There are a couple of things I want to discuss," he said. "The first of these is, what thought have you given to your title?" The question really threw me. With all the problems there were to tackle, concern for a title was the least of my worries.

"I really haven't given it any thought, Ted."

"Well," Rogers replied, "I've been giving it quite a good deal of thought. The closest thing to your position up to now has been called mail order sales manager. But I feel your title should be much more encompassing and meaningful and carry much more stature."

Out of a group of titles, all suggested by Rogers, he thought the most impressive was that of "director of mail marketing." It sounded all right to me and I told him so. Then he started vacillating, like a merchant who will bargain himself down when his quotation of a price goes unchallenged. He kept arguing with himself until I finally said, "Ted, I really couldn't care less, director of mail marketing is just fine." We left it at that.

That first day at Playboy just wasn't my day. But then

again, neither were the following nine days. After about two weeks my immediate staff, people I had brought with me from Whitney-Forbes or Cowles, told me I had made a mistake "because these people are not like us."

What they meant was our shared belief that what you do in life is to determine your objective and then go after it until you accomplish it. Then you look around for another objective. It's a basic outlook but one strongly embraced by myself and the men who followed me to Playboy. By now we knew that the people at Playboy did not share any such belief.

But there was something else we all felt—the unhealthy atmosphere that prevailed. It was a stink in the air around executives we had to deal with—the stink of fear. Because they were afraid, grossly afraid, of Hefner and what he'd think of any decision they made or any action they took.

Listen in on a typical conversation:

"Which approach do you think is better," I'd ask, "A or B?"

"A is better."

"Then why are we using B?"

"Because several years ago, Hefner said he liked B."

I'd go through it again with another executive and his reason would be "because I think if we were to put the question to Hefner he would say that he likes B better." And maybe a third man would say, "We're using B because in my dreams I got a vague glimmer that if someone were once to have asked Hefner or were to ask him in the future he would say B. So just on the slight contingency that that's so, I'm going to stick with B."

That last is hypothetical, but it's based on real happenings. These things occur at Playboy, with grown men, supposedly responsible professionals, who do it the second-class way because Hefner, they think, prefers it that way. Ask them if they've ever told Hefner this and they say no. Ask them why and they say they're afraid to.

This is real, hard-core sickness. It is the kind of corporate malady that is virtually incurable because to cure it involves

59

drastic change, not in operational methods but in human character. Usually the only cure is a transfusion of all new people.

Even if this condition does exist, "So what?" would be a likely response from anyone familiar with Playboy's astounding growth in 18 years. Except for a slight setback in 1954, Playboy has been a financial winner from its very first issue in 1953. Any company that has grown from a deficit of $23,000 with revenues of $268,000 in 1954 to net earnings of $9,221,000 with revenues of $131,586,000 in fiscal 1971 can't be that sick. Can it? Sick things just don't grow like that. But maybe Playboy is a phenomenon that has managed to grow in spite of itself.

Playboy was a potent catalyst in the sexual revolution that exploded in the late fifties and sixties. The momentum of that explosion carried Playboy with it. Hefner's timing was perfect—Playboy was the right thing at the right time.

Given the same circumstances, however, with a different management situation, maybe that $131 million would now be $200 million or $300 million. I'm not sure. But of one thing I am sure. If something can grow despite an ailment, it should grow better once that ailment is cured.

Anyway, my staff recognized the weak management situation and asked me what I intended to do about it. I had no real choice. Leaving Playboy was the only sensible thing to do. I felt responsible for the support of a lot of families in that group, dubbed "Byer's Jewish Mafia" by one Playboy executive.

I started looking around and not long after found a favorable situation. I was set to join Plaza Group, a New York-based direct mail merchandising firm that was publicly held. I would head up a newly-formed subsidiary to be called Plaza-Byer. All the arrangements were made within a few months. I was ready to sign the papers when I talked with Preuss late one evening.

"By the way," he said, "I want you to know that Hefner and I are impressed with what you've been doing. We think you are probably the single, most valuable personnel find ever to come to this company, with the possible exception of myself. We think there are other things for you here and all you have to do is . . . well, we have to discuss it and see what it is."

I really felt like a traitor, then, so I moved up my timetable by about a month and said, "Well, look, Bob, I wasn't going to say this until about three or four weeks from now but I'm planning to leave."

"What do you mean?" he asked. "Why?"

"I'm leaving because of the bunch of sickies around here. I can't stand having to deal with them. These people are wallowing in their own ignorance and that's brought out by this hideous fear of doing something contrary to what they think Hefner wants, or thinks."

"God," Preuss said, "you can't leave, we need you."

"No," I told him, "you don't need me, you'll get along without me and forget I was ever here."

Well, he evidently told Hefner because in the next several weeks I couldn't buy a meal for myself; every lunch, every dinner, I was with Rosenzweig or Preuss or Spectorsky or with Arnold Morton. It started to wear me down. The constant handholding and cajoling finally led to a meeting with Hefner, who asked, "What will it take to keep you here?"

"Nothing," I answered, "I don't want to stay here, this is a sick company."

"Well," he said, "tell me how to make it better and be a part of making it better."

He was upset. Walking out on him was an ego affront, for one thing. It also meant losing someone who had improved the quality of the direct response advertising in a short time—the very reason I was hired.

I concentrated on Hefner's words, "making it better," and replied, "No, I don't think so, because I don't want to waste my time and effort and future trying to build a solid edifice on a fundamentally weak base."

"Why, what do you mean?" he asked, although he must have known the answer.

"I mean," I said, with some heat, "that since I've been

61

here I've seen a greater abdication of responsibility than in all the rest of my years in business. Do you know that executives here are doing things in what they know is an inferior way because they think it will be acceptable to you or Preuss or Morton? And if key people are doing it, what are their underlings doing? That's why I say this company is sick and that's why I don't want to waste my time trying to hypo it."

Hefner began sucking on his pipe more vigorously, perhaps wanting to stall a few moments to mull over what I had just said. His response was direct and quite unexpected: "I know some of these people are weaklings. Suppose I gave you the authority to ferret them out and to replace them with better people?"

"That would be a start," I blurted. Now I was the one who needed time for mulling because I was beginning to think about staying. The meeting started at three in the afternoon and lasted until midnight. It took all that time to work out the ground rules under which I would stay.

I was to become the corporate director of marketing and a vice president, as well as an additional member of the seven-man executive committee. This is ostensibly a policy-making board but it really is a meaningless echo. Every issue that comes up for a vote gets unanimous approval. At that time, however, I didn't realize how ineffectual it was. It only met twice while I was there.

We agreed that Ted Rogers, whom I was replacing as marketing director, was to be placed in another position because Hefner felt he could not fire him. After all, Ted had several ex-wives, he had to support his fourth wife—and he was a friend of Spectorsky's. Rogers became director of entertainment, a newly-created position. (He left Playboy last February, one week after Spectorsky's death.)

Other conditions to which Hefner agreed were that I was to be given a favorable option price on 17,000 shares of Playboy stock; my salary was to be increased from $100,000 to $200,000 a year, and I was to have complete responsibility for all advertising, promotion, public relations, corporate development and most sales activity. The only exception to anything I requested was in connection with Howard Lederer, who was advertising director. It was thought that he should have a long breaking-in period before reporting to anyone other than Hefner. He'd always resisted reporting even to Preuss.

The major ingredient in my staying was implicit in the premise on which Hefner and I had started this talk. I had his authority to do as I saw fit with various personnel, even if it meant letting people go who had been there for many years. Only after a thorough analysis of the circumstances would such action be taken. I promised myself I would never abuse my responsibilities—nor would I shy away from them.

A memorable midnight—suddenly I was a marketing director and a vice president of Playboy at age 28. At last in my career I had reached a position that would allow me to seek remedies for those diseases I believed to be crippling to a corporation. I was elated.

But along with the elation, the sense of achievement, there was the sobering knowledge of what a corporate director of marketing should be and do—or at least, what I had to be and do to satisfy my own standards.

Somewhere in Playboy's files is a lengthy memo in which I first defined the duties of a marketing director and then elaborated on the philosophy and psychology he must follow. It was heavy stuff, but it also helped me to define my objectives and to assess just how vital my role at Playboy was.

The overall responsibility, I said, was to establish policy, give direction, coordinate and supervise elements involved in the marketing of our products and services. This included product and market development, sales development and procedures, research, product and/or service quality and performance, and supervision of media and other channels through which the product or service is communicated to the market (advertising, promotion, publicity).

As the person of final accountability, I considered it my job to make certain the company, through all methods of market communication, spoke with one voice. I anticipated minimal conflict as to how goods or services were advertised and marketed. But a consistent standard of quality, taste and image must emerge from the sum total of all the company's marketing activities.

Other requirements were to establish a high level of professionalism in the execution of marketing policies; to carefully assess the needs of the company in terms of cohesive structure, rather than autonomous divisions and areas; and to provide the necessary qualified personnel and organization procedures to execute these functions.

But to fulfill these basic duties, a marketing director must keep constantly aware of other factors. The smoothness of his relationship to the divisions and subsidiaries, for instance, is based solely on open lines of communication, plus mutual respect. Otherwise, the relationship will be confused, meaningless and unrewarding.

Through my close contacts with marketing directors in other multi-divisional companies, I have learned a good deal as to how they do—and do not—function. I must repeat that it is very much dependent on respect for and understanding of the marketing function as to whether or not the corporate marketing director will contribute as he should.

If, however, there is a lack of this understanding, if there is an unconscious protectiveness present within a division, then human relationships are usually not sufficient to overcome the deficiencies.

What it boils down to is this: a corporate marketing function can only contribute to a division what the division will let it.

I knew that my job was not going to be an easy one—but that was the challenge.

Part of the challenge, too, was doing the job well enough to justify a $200,000 salary, second only to Hefner's. Considering what I had done for Playboy up until that night, and the contributions I might make in my new role, was I worth it?

I thought so.

So did Hefner.

Chapter 5
Shrinking The Shrink

Charlie M., a physically small individual who is somewhat intense, might have thought I was out to get him not long after my promotion.

Theo Frederick set up a luncheon with Dr. Charles M., an industrial psychologist, to update my shrink audit, which provided the introduction to this book.

The shrink audit is a big thing at Playboy and highly confidential, at least as far as the victim is concerned. It is given to members of Playboy's management corps. But it is reserved for only the eyes of the executive elite. When Charlie realized that I had seen mine, he was surprised and a bit uneasy. It was understandable. After all, I knew what he thought he knew about me. And perhaps he thought I resented his analysis. On some points I did.

I had first met Charlie shortly after I started working at Playboy. Following a series of psychological tests I was to be interviewed for an hour or so by a psychologist. The test results coupled with the observations from the interview constituted the audit, or the conclusions based upon Charlie's

65

analysis. Because 1 am wary of shrinks, when Charlie called me to make an appointment for the interview I figured, dammit, he's not going to waste my valuable work day. If he wants to interview me he'll have to do it at 6 a.m.

"That's right, 6 a.m. in your office, doctor," 1 insisted. There was a slight pause, a clearing of the throat and, "Uh, that's rather early, don't you think?" Dr. M. asked. 1 sort of baffled Charlie by what he thought was my eccentricity in insisting on the 6 a.m. meeting time. But I really told him the truth, it wasn't eccentricity, it wasn't for effect. 1 didn't have to impress him.

Incidentally, mine was one of the few cases of a prospect for an executive position not being audited prior to acceptance. And that's the ironic part. If I had been audited, Hefner might very well have said, "No, don't hire Byer." But what's in a shrink audit, anyway? It is just part of Playboy's idea of being professionals in management. They don't use the audits properly because they end up in the hands of laymen who haven't the slightest understanding of what they mean or how they should be used. Hefner, Preuss, Theo and Rosenzweig read mine, probably with the curiosity of little old ladies peeping out of the window at the neighbors— "Look at that, girls, they're fighting again."

That initial interview, for which Charlie arrived promptly at 6 a.m., lasted for nearly six hours. It had become intriguing to the point that I had forgotten my original purpose of zipping through it and getting to work. When we parted Charlie had pages of written notes. He had learned quite a lot about me but I learned a few things about him, too. For instance, in the course of conversation about my background and earnings, he naturally asked, "What were your earnings last year?" When I told him $246,000 he said, "Oh, well I'm about $150,000 a year myself." (Playboy, incidentally, was paying Charlie $300 for each shrink report.)

"Why tell me about your annual income?" I earnestly asked.

"I just feel you will respond better to those you consider your equals," he earnestly answered.

66

"No," I said, "I don't think that's why at all. I think you feel insecure because of something I've been saying and are trying to prove to me that you are my equal—not that you are, Charlie. Isn't that right?"

My response was merely resentment of Dr. M.'s judgment regarding my values. But I felt better after saying it even if I was spouting nonsense off the top of my head. Surprisingly, however, Charlie didn't see it that way. He took his glasses off and with an introspective gaze said, "I'm sorry, I think you may be right. Each of us periodically suffers some level of insecurity and sometimes it may show more than others." Somehow I couldn't believe what I was hearing. Sure, I appreciated Charlie's honesty in 'fessing up on the spot. But at the same time, I was forced to wonder: "Why is this guy interviewing ME?"

Now, several months later, Charlie and I were at it again. Theo, I suppose, was there to back him up. When he heard me reciting passages from my audit, he sat there looking at me like I might suddenly grab a fork and stab him in the carotid artery. At that moment he probably looked at Theo as a witness rather than a luncheon companion. He didn't even ask how I had gotten hold of my audit. He just sat there, listening and fidgeting in his chair. I don't think he had much of an appetite that day.

While I put a different interpretation on some points in my shrink audit, there is really only one on which I disagree. The point is stated several times in different ways. I do not believe that I am "a self-serving person who is indifferent to the needs of other people," or that I have "little loyalty to anyone other than myself," or that I "expect more of other people than I am prepared to give in return."

And what Charlie calls "liabilities," my being materialistic and acquisitive—I think they are the most basic assets anyone can have. I think here is a clue to the personality of Charlie. It appears he has a fundamental Protestant ethic that makes him view acquisitiveness and materialism as negatives.

Even Hefner would have taken issue with Dr. M. on that point. After all, these so-called "liabilities" are the basis of what Playboy is really all about. Hefner's comment to Charlie would have been the one he made in a 1970 *Esquire* interview: "Our entire puritan culture insists that what will *not* make you happy is material wealth and pleasures of the flesh. But . . . maybe it is a significant part of what *will* make you happy. What's really worthwhile, they used to try to tell us, is hard work and suffering, because in the next world, Charlie, it'll all work out for you. What it was was a very good technique to keep the workers happy in their lousy place."

After hearing that, Charlie might then have asked Hefner: "If that's truly how you feel, why do you work so hard? Why for so many years did you incarcerate yourself in the bowels of that mansion working 36-hour shifts while gulping down Pepsis and as many as 35 Dexedrine pills a day to keep going? When you finally did emerge from your Howard Hughesian isolation in 1969, you were gaunt and haggard, 40 pounds lighter, a mere shell of a man. All for what?

"If that isn't 'hard work' and 'suffering' then I don't know what is. And by the way, Mr. Hefner, I could construe from all this that you, too, are among 'the workers happy in their lousy place.' "

To all this Hefner would simply reply: "It is not work per se, but the fact that I enjoy what I am doing."

And as for his isolation, Hefner sees that as "more physical than mental." He says his house serves to eliminate the day-to-day time-wasting routines everyone goes through. It separates him from "wasted motions" such as commuting, going out for lunch, and even the most routine of all—dressing.

For Hefner it all adds up to self-fulfillment, the product of which is happiness with a capital H.

But as I got to know Hefner better, I realized it would take more than making money and the enjoyment of doing his own thing to make him happy. His objectives are very purposeful and specific regarding his life and identity. Hefner wants to be known as a serious businessman who has shaped the life styles of other people. Until he achieves that recognition, he will never by fully satisfied and he admits it.

"Wealth and success in business are all fine," Hefner once told me, adding emphatically, "but I'm mainly concerned with Playboy's impact on society." And where Hefner's business savvy is concerned, he readily admits that he has trouble reading a profit and loss statement. But he still considers himself a "very bright guy and good at business, at getting at the core and picking out flaws." And that he certainly is, as I was to learn.

This anxiety for recognition in the business community is shared equally by the other Playboy executives. Arnold Morton summed it up in an interview in *Executive Magazine* when he said: "I don't think we have had our due in the financial world. In the next few years we're going to be recognized as businessmen. A little of that Playboy stuff falls through the cracks all the time. Hefner is going to be proved not only one of the creative young men of the world, but he's going to be building one of the great business empires." Morton made that statement about a year before I joined Playboy.

As for Hefner's identity, just read a *Playboy* magazine. Any issue will do because the magazine is Hefner's personal statement in terms of what the good life is. The magazine over the years has, of course, rendered far more of the good life than Hefner himself has lived. For that matter, it renders more of the good life than any man can live unless he is a full-time playboy. But if all he does with his life is play then Hefner would hardly consider him a playboy.

"What is a playboy?" the magazine asked rhetorically in 1956 when it was three years old. It answered: "Is he simply a wastrel, a ne'er-do-well, a fashion bum? Far from it: he can be a sharp-minded young business executive, a worker in the arts, a university professor, an architect or engineer. He can be many things, provided he possesses a certain *point of view*. He must see life not as a vale of tears, but as a happy time; he must take joy in his work, without regarding it as the end and all of living; he must be an alert man, an aware man, a man of taste, a man sensitive to pleasure, a man who—without acquiring the stigma of the voluptuary or dilettante—can live life to the hilt. This is the sort of man we mean when we use the word playboy."

(Incidentally, at that time *Playboy's* average reader was 29.6 years old, earning $8,150 a year. And among its then 230,000 subscribers, 41.3 percent had an executive-professional business title or position.)

Hefner originally decided on the word playboy because of its infrequent usage and its dated overtones suggesting the Roaring Twenties. In the old sense he saw the playboy as a limited part of society. He set out to resurrect the playboy in men as a major part of their lives. And as Hefner explained to *Esquire*: "From the beginning it (the magazine) has been more generalized than my own life, but very much related to the things that I aspire to and enjoy and from which a person could pick and choose . . ."

So, Charlie, there is some method to Hefner's madness as well as to mine.

There is some truth in Charlie's obervation that I am "much more likely to operate on sudden insight and intuition than facts and logic." But I think he makes a serious error in lumping together "facts and logic." After all, one need not have a command of the facts in order to make logical conclusions.

Charlie finally did ask me how I obtained the audit. "I got it from Preuss on a temporary loan-out," I said. With that he turned to Theo and in his very best "I told you so" tone he said, "See, Theo, I was right. The fact that Steve obtained a copy of his report shows his inability to abide by the rules of a corporate framework." He also was somewhat miffed with Preuss. Theo just sat there nodding her head in affirmation.

Our luncheon ended shortly after that. Charlie suggested that we meet again in a few months to see how my new position was agreeing with me. But Charlie couldn't fool me. I was sure he wanted to meet only to corroborate other observations he had made portending my future at Playboy. We parted amicably.

Chapter 6
The Pecking Order

"Three new executive appointments in Playboy Enterprises have been announced by Hugh M. Hefner, president.

"They are a direct result of Playboy's increasing growth, he explained, and are designed to meet the future corporate needs of both HMH Publishing Co., Inc., publishers of Playboy *magazine and parent organization of a number of subsidiary enterprises, and Playboy Clubs International, Inc., currently operating 19 Playboy Clubs and Playboy Club-Hotels in the U.S., Canada, Jamaica and England.*

"Edward A. (Ted) Rogers was named . . . "

So began the news release Playboy put out officially announcing my appointment as vice president and corporate director of marketing. It also announced Rogers in his new role of vice president, director of entertainment and Nelson Futch as vice president, director of public relations.

That news release also served as my official introduction to the Playboy pecking order. One of my first acts as a top

71

executive was to let myself be downgraded in the news releases and in the internal memos notifying the staff of the change in my position.

"Everybody will know you have deposed Rogers," Preuss said, "but will you let him save face by appearing first in the news release and memo?"

At first I thought Preuss was joking and I waited momentarily for a smile or even a sardonic grin. But he was dead serious. I decided to play it straight; the fact that Rogers' name came before mine was incidental.

"I really couldn't care less, Bob. I've accomplished what I wanted to. The sequence of names in a release or a memo mean nothing to me."

But, of course, the word got out fast that Monday morning through the grapevine. You could practically hear the hissing sound of the whispers. And the doorman clicked his heels and everybody I met—the elevator starter, the secretaries—was buttering me up. (One girl on each floor was responsible for distributing mass media announcements; department announcements were distributed through interoffice mail.)

I really first became aware of the high level of finesse with which status symbols and executive poise were treated at Playboy on my first day there. Preuss had asked if I would move onto the third floor, which he was planning to convert to additional space for Playboy. It had just been taken over from its various tenants. The request was simple enough and I was happy to do it. All I wanted was an office big enough to walk around in, with some basic ingredients, such as a desk and a table and some chairs. I was asked to specify "precisely" what I wanted and that's when a ridiculous episode started.

"I want a conference table where I can sit and work and meet other people. I don't like dealing with somebody across a desk. In fact, you can leave the desk out and just give me a conference table," I said to Preuss' assistant, Lance Hooper.

Hooper is to Preuss what Rosenzweig is to Hefner—and then some. He joined Playboy in July 1967, giving up a partnership in the firm of Hooper and Ihlenfeld, certified public accountants, in Manitowoc, Wisconsin. He, like Rosenzweig, carries the title of vice president (of finance). Like Rosenzweig, he is a trusty assistant whose loyalty to his master is beyond question. But that's where the similarities end. Hooper, about 50 years old, has a ruddy complexion and sports a gray-haired crew cut. Dressed in gabardine suits and button-down-collar shirts, he is anything but mod. He lacks warmth. I always had the feeling that Hooper was lurking in the shadows with a pencil and a pad noting my moves. He was always dashing off memos to Preuss about the actions of some executive or some situation he had happened upon.

But for now I was dealing with Hooper on a different level, as man to man.

"How large a conference table do you want, Steve?" asked Lance.

"I don't care. What sizes do they come in?"

"Well," he answered, "they come 36, 42, 48, 56 and 72 inches in diameter."

"Fine, give me a 72-inch one."

"Oh," he said, "I'm sorry but you have to be a vice president to get a conference table 72 inches in diameter."

"Then why did you ask me?"

"I just thought you might select one of the others," he said.

That comment sort of aggravated me. There it was again—the pettiness of corporate bureaucracy, this time edging me away from the table. Rather than pout, I bellowed, "Just because I'm not a vice president doesn't mean that I don't meet with groups of four or five or six people. I want a 72-inch table."

This naturally resulted in a Hooper-to-Preuss memo regarding my request for a 72-inch conference table. It stated that since Preuss, of course, knew that the 72-inch tables were reserved only for vice presidents and above, would he agree to make an exception in Byer's case. If he didn't agree, then would he please advise me so. Preuss called me to his office.

"Steve, are you sure you need a 72-inch conference table?" Preuss asked, eyeing his shiny 72-inch conference table with the pride of a kid who was the first on his block to get a two-wheeler.

What nonsense, I thought. This matter already has wasted much valuable time. Then and there I decided to make my stand.

"Bob, if there's an 84-inch conference table that's what I want. And if there isn't, but there is a 72-inch, I guess I want the 72."

And that's how I got my out-of-the-pecking-order 72-inch conference table, because Preuss agreed to make an exception. That had required a total of about 10 minutes of our time, about 20 minutes with Hooper, about 15 or 20 minutes of Hooper's time writing the memo and five minutes of Preuss' time reading it. All of that because a 72-inch conference table was reserved for vice presidents and above only.

I also discovered that an effort is made to maintain equality within each management level or strata. None of this had anything to do with function or with need, other than the emotional need of proving at what level you were. Only Morton and Preuss, for instance, had built-in entertainment-monitoring sections (color TV-stereo), wet-bars and refrigerators.

Even what went on the floors was "ranked." Morton, Preuss and Spectorsky had carpeting that not only was different than the lush "Spicepoint" used throughout the reception areas and other offices, but different from each other. And Vincent T. Tajiri, photography editor who left recently, had a little patch of parquet under his chair behind his desk—I suppose in deference to his years there. Light boxes, used to study photographic transparencies, were another thing—if you rated one. It was either a built-in or one of those cheesy little ones that you stand up on a counter top. So many stupid things like that, you couldn't count them.

So there came to be a real trauma on Hooper's part because I agreed to move to the third floor to an office that previously had been the advertising sales office of *Esquire* magazine. It was a huge room that had been occupied by one man and his secretary. He had never put up a wall, he just paneled the whole damn room and then put in cabinetry and cupboards. So they were going to put in a wall that blocked off a 12-by-16-foot section of it because my title allowed me only a 12-by-16 office.

My secretary and I were to be the only ones, temporarily, in this room. Yet, they were eager to put up two walls abutting two other walls to make an office that was in line with my title, even though the rest of it was empty. I said this was ridiculous and the maintenance crew started arguing. No matter what I said they insisted they had to block out an office because all executives at Playboy have offices. That's one of the great things about Playboy.

Finally I told them to go ahead. As soon as they left, I pulled the conference table into the other area, which was larger, and now my office was 20 by 60 feet, less 12 by 16. Anyway, it was really quite a great office, it was big and it had a private bathroom and it was just fine.

This was my initiation into the pecking order at Playboy. But there are many, many examples of it—who rides in the limousine to and from the airport or can have a visitor picked up at the airport in the limousine; who flies first class instead of coach; who carries the air travel card that's good for international travel, not just domestic; who stays in suites in hotels, not single rooms; who receives the $225-a-month allowance for the company car and who the $165.

But there was even a pecking order among those at the top of the corporate pecking order. For example, it was an elite group that received the higher allowance for automobiles. And a lot of it had to do with how much you knew and whether or not you walked into Preuss' office screaming, "I just found out there's a higher allowance bla-bla-bla."

However, I was not considered quite as high up in the pecking order, in terms of title, as Spectorsky and Morton, because they were senior vice presidents. They were not considered as high up as Preuss. But none of the other vice presidents in the corporation or the PCI subsidiary were considered as high up in the pecking order as I was.

And there were other ingredients. Michael Demarest,

former executive editor, was a man who was so totally conscious of pecking order that he almost resigned, immediately after joining the company, over the order in which the names appeared on the *Playboy* masthead. Demarest, 47, had been a 17-year *Time* magazine staffer prior to joining *Playboy*. He would not agree to art director Art Paul's name appearing on the same level as his own. Mike threatened to resign and he finally won.

But none of them had their own washroom. Hooper was upset that somebody might discover my temporary quarters on the third floor had a bathroom. Having your own clothes closet also was a big deal.

There were other things—who rode in the Big Bunny, who was invited to the Mansion parties, who could give away the corporate Christmas gifts, who went on the special trips like the golf outing to La Costa (California) for Hefner's birthday party.

Expense accounts were very tight for non-executive employees and very liberal for top executives. You could write off almost anything if you were a high-bracket executive. It was absolutely incredible how much chicanery went on.

One executive, for example, decided to accept an invitation to speak before the Mail Advertising Club of Honolulu. So he went to Honolulu, spoke for ten minutes, stayed for ten days, and wrote off the entire trip as a business expense.

The rationale he used was that he was considering new sites for Playboy clubs or hotels, he was thinking about that entire marketing area, he was establishing good will with potential advertisers and so on.

He bluffed his way through it and Preuss told me afterwards that he either had to call the man a liar or let it go by with a warning. He decided to warn him. I remember Preuss telling me that the trip cost more than $3,000.

Now, if it is true that imitation is the sincerest form of flattery, Hefner is among the most flattered men alive today, because his executives are a case of monkey see, monkey do. Such devout emulation added at least two more elements to the pecking order. One I called "musical offices" and the other the "carbon business." Both are widely played.

Anyone who wants to see Hefner has to go to the Mansion and that sets the tone to musical offices. Some executives tested their status in the pecking order by who came to them. An executive going to the office of a subordinate would be like the owner of a plantation sitting down to dinner in his slave's shack. After an executive mastered the game within his department, he was ready for the big leagues—the intramural class, so to speak. That is, bucking status with your counterpart in another department.

If an editorial executive had to meet with a marketing bigwig, in whose office would the meeting take place? After all, such a meeting would also entail leaving one's domain because those departments were on different floors. What a coup for the one whose office was used!

The carbon business was a bit more subtle. Again Hefner himself set the stage. Of Hefner, *The Chicago Daily News* once piously observed: "Corporations don't run themselves while the president locks himself in the bedroom and studies nude pictures." Then how does a president run his company from the confines of his boudoir with limited personal contact with members of his management team? The long memo—that's how. It has been his main link for years.

Hefner is a memo writer if there ever was. Some of his memos have run as long as thirty typewritten pages covering important points and sometimes trivial ones. So the others also write long memos. And consequently the carbon business has found its way into the pecking order.

If one executive wants to impress his peers with his knowledge of a given subject, he sends out carbons of a memo he has written. It also became a political thing. For instance, if someone wanted to impress the person to whom the memo was written, he carboned Hefner on it or Preuss or both. That was a classy memo.

At some companies this kind of thing manifests itself by blind carbons but at Playboy it's open—are you important enough to carbon Hefner? So goes the carbon business, a beautiful plum for name droppers.

So even top executives took extraordinary advantage of their place in the pecking order. This is another situation at Playboy—that is, the way the execs are so protective of their "rights" and so fearful somebody will get something they don't. I'd be the last to deny that rank has its privileges.

Chapter 7
On The Firing Line

Rain pelted the runway as the 707 sat gently down on Chicago's O'Hare field. It was 2 a.m. and the world's busiest airport was pausing to catch its breath. The place was desolate. Cabs were so scarce that I had to share one with two other people for the fifteen-mile trip to the city. One of the passengers was a woman who worked for a marketing research firm. We began talking about each other's businesses and it turned into an enlightening ride.

"Playboy!" the woman chirped when I told her who I worked for. "Were you there when that young guy came in and changed the whole place? He fired a mass of people and changed so many things there!" I couldn't believe what I was hearing. She was obviously talking about me.

"If I mentioned that young guy's name do you think you'd know it?" I asked.

"I'm sure I would. They say he's a terror."

"Is it Byer, Stephen Byer, by any chance?"

"That's it, that's the name," she said. "Do you know him?"

"Yes, ma'am, I know him very well. I'm Stephen Byer."

"Oh, my gosh," she said, "oh, I'm terribly sorry," and she was stammering away. I smiled and let her off the hook by changing the subject.

Suddenly I felt like a dignitary or a celebrity of sorts. Here it was two in the morning and it tickled me that I could meet somebody who responded to my name the way she did. My feelings were somewhat ambivalent. On one hand, my reputation was that of a free-swinging, heartless axe man bent on clearing the deadwood out of Playboy. On the other hand, however, I was an individual accomplishing something big at Playboy. And that was important, too.

But when you get right down to it, it wasn't really such a "mass" of people I fired during the purge or reign of terror, as it has been described. One of my conditions when I became marketing director related to my concern about the personnel situation. Hefner agreed that I could alter it as I saw fit in attempting to make the company better.

I set about doing so the Monday morning I came in as marketing director. I called Theo Frederick and told her I wanted, by the time I left for New York on Wednesday, the personnel files, salary sheets, the initial questionnaire filled in by incoming employees, of everyone within my areas. She said she would be unable to get that much detail within a day or two. I then decided to start with the highest-ranking personnel, twenty or so of the key executives within the areas of advertising, public relations, promotion, mail marketing, Playboy products and Playboy Preferred. I reviewed the files during my trip and when I returned to Chicago, I began discussions with the executives concerned.

The talks resulted in the eventual firing of approximately forty to fifty people at a combined annual salary of nearly a half-million dollars over a four-month period, beginning in April of 1970.

I suppose firing forty to fifty, out of a staff of about one hundred, is a lot in a relatively short period, but everything was getting done more efficiently and faster.

Now, take that payroll and add the overhead and the total

is a great deal more than a half-million dollars. Maybe the salaries are $400,000 or $420,000. The general formula for overhead, for office space and supplies, telephones, electricity, equipment, fringe benefits, Social Security and insurance and others—generalized figures are 25 to 40 percent of salary. It amounted to quite a sum the company was being saved. But nobody seemed to think of that.

The first reaction I got from the executive level was from Theo Frederick, who expressed incredulity and asked me if I really had cleared the dismissals with Hefner. I said, "Theo, is this really your concern?" But it eventually occurred to me that it was her concern because she had been the personnel director responsible, at least in part, for the hiring of all these people. And perhaps the dismissals put her in a bad light.

The second response came from Preuss, who told me that morale was terrible and that people were coming to him "in droves" to complain that they were insecure in their jobs. I told him I was certain morale was bad among those who knew or could guess they were about to be fired. I asked him if any of the people in whom I had confidence had come to him and he said no.

The third was Lance Hooper, who told me that a few people had been in to see him, asking what the hell was going on, why all these people were being fired. "Just tell them to ask me, Lance," I advised him. I would have fired even more if I had been able to find satisfactory replacements.

Hefner's reaction to the firings was that he had heard some rumblings but he wasn't concerned about them.

Incidentally, I seldom fired anyone until he had been given a second chance, so to speak. The procedure I followed was to have a lengthy talk with the individual in order to evaluate job function or to determine if there were any problems I was unaware of. If there was a question regarding a person's capability, I assigned work loads that I felt would test their ability. Only then would I make my decision to keep someone or not.

There also were the underground vibrations. I got filthy anonymous notes in the inter-office mail, cartoons indicating someone being fired and an obscene phone call at 2:30 one morning. But I ignored them since none of them threatened bodily harm.

So there were all those things, and more, during that period, along with constant talk about the firings. But there was no mention of how clearing out all this deadwood was saving the company a half-million dollars and more.

The ubiquitous "they" questioned how I could, heartless wretch that I am, let go a woman who had given seven years of her life to the company? This was the woman who, when asked to produce a compendium of her most successful work for Playboy, brought in a portfolio of her work from 1965 to 1968. I asked her what she had done from February 1968 to 1970 and she said she had nothing she felt was quite as good as her earlier work.

"Well," I said, "do you feel you have earned your way in the last two years?"

"Yes," she replied, "because I make a great many phone calls every day. I'm on the phone constantly with the advertising salesmen, for one thing, telling them how many pieces of promotional material are left in the inventory at any given time."

"Don't you think that $26,000 a year is a little high to be paying an inventory card?" I asked her.

"Well," she said, "I'm more than just an inventory card because inventory cards aren't kept up that accurately and that currently. The salesmen want to know that there are 2,000 fashion form brochures, say, in stock on Monday and not only 1,800. I let them know these things."

It wasn't just $26,000 for her, it was also $8,000 for her assistant and secretary. I fired both of them.

People kept questioning the validity of letting someone go—like a copywriter who had not submitted a piece of copy in eighteen months that was used for an ad or promotional effort. Or a designer whose work had been redone constantly by the head art director during his entire time with the company.

So the gossip and the hearsay and the rumors centered

around all these people being let go, all of the petty reasons and petty judgments that come up when a person is fired. Multiply it by the rumor mill that exists at Playboy. Then multiply it again by virtue of the people who are generally just insecure about their positions from start to finish, and all of it came out as though this beast was terrorizing the Playboy organization.

I got this not just from inside but from outside. The tales came back to me about how many people were being fired and it became tremendously exaggerated, of course—all of a sudden there were more people being fired than there were on the staff.

But pruning of personnel was not the only way I was able to cut costs. The second major area was in the wastefulness of the internal staff. For example, the staff photographers. They shot thousands and thousands of unnecessary and unusable films of Playmates. And every time they shot a Playmate or a prospective Playmate, they also shot this girl posed for what they thought were promotional purposes. The result was never used, because it was done in such an amateurish, bumbling fashion. So I cut this expensive, don't-give-a-damn, Playboy's-got-plenty-of-money habit to more reasonable proportions. Film and its processing cost too much to waste.

Another drain on Playboy's corporate pocket that I was able to stop up was in duplicate mailing lists for key club member promotions.

Before my time, they sent mailings to credit card holders of American Express, Diner's Club, and Carte Blanche; to their own Playboy Club keyholders and *Playboy* magazine subscribers and to many others, all at the same time.

"This is ridiculous," I said when I discovered it, "look at the heavy duplication on these lists. Let's take the most productive one and we'll get most of the people who are on the other lists, or at least a goodly percentage of them." So that's what we did and we sold as many keys as had been sold when solicitations were sent to all of the names on all of the lists.

In 1971 they went back to the old approach. I received

five samples of the identical promotional package within a two-day period.

This waste is no penny-ante proposition. One year they sent mailings to all 600,000 Carte Blanche credit card holders; all 750,000 Diner's Club members; a high percentage of the nearly 3,000,000 American Express card holders; 4,300,000 (through several offers) to *Playboy* magazine subscribers; 30,000 to Evergreen Club; 250,000 to TWA credit card holders; 46,000 to EDP managers; 40,000 to buyers of John Surrey cigars; several 45,000 test groups to various lists; 200,000 to inquiries and referrals—these are people who write in and inquire about securing a key or whose names are submitted by others as those who might be interested in a key—and 320,000 to house lists.

The cost of this mailing, about $1,200,000, is beyond belief and is because Playboy pays so much more for everything than anyone else does. For printing a letter, Playboy can pay $6 for every thousand pieces when others are paying $3 or $4. This is because Playboy's buyers of printed matter are not very dollar-conscious. Anyone who calls on Playboy knows that if he plays his cards right he can charge twice as much as he would elsewhere and still get the order. Playboy is known for being the softest touch in Chicago for printed matter. So, at Playboy's costs, it would be around $140-145 per thousand pieces for various promotional efforts that would cost anyone else between $110 and $120. Take that times the millions of pieces of mail released and you get some inkling of the massive amount of money spent on these mailings.

Speaking of mailing lists, Hefner had the oddest slant on them for *Playboy* subscription solicitations. It was utter nonsense. He wanted no outside lists used to get subscriptions because he felt that was "forcing" circulation. In his mind only the present *Playboy* subscribers and keyholders are the true life's blood of the magazine. "Look," he said, "since we have been going after subscriptions with more and more inserts and envelopes and ads in the magazine, it's true we've been getting in more subscribers but these people haven't been renewing as well. Why? Because they aren't the hard core of subscribers who will continue reading and re-subscribing to the magazine year after year."

It's true, at that time renewals from current subscribers were high. Now, I think, they're down to about 38 percent. But even a 60 percent rate, which few magazines get, meant Playboy had to pick up the lost 40 percent in new subscribers or newsstand sales. That's what Hefner was forgetting. Re-newals are important because that's where a magazine really makes its money on subscription circulation. If you don't pick up new readers somewhere you lose circulation and, consequently, advertising income.

So when I persisted that we needed to try something new, like outside lists, Hefner reluctantly agreed to go along with it. I began sending subscription mailings to airline credit card holders, American Express names, and so on. The results were what I expected. We were able to acquire new sub-scribers at virtually no cost, because the mailings paid for themselves.

Another part of my new job, I realized, meant bucking Hefner and his chorus of yes-men. I once said the loudest sounds at Playboy were those of necks creaking as heads nodded automatically to whatever Hefner said.

But when I talked to Hefner about what a sick company it was, I was shortsighted. I thought the problem lay with the people who work for Hefner but the truth is they simply reflect the top man himself. I mean, Hefner yesses himself instead of ever questioning himself. It's obvious he recognizes that an executive corps of yes-men has grown up around him. When mistakes are made, there is no ranting or raving. Why should there be? In essence, the mistakes are Hefner's.

An *Esquire* interviewer once asked Hefner about the people who make mistakes. The exchange went like this:

Esquire: "But this huge empire you've got—it must be full of people who screw up and things like that?"

Hefner: "Of course there are. The higher up they get, as a matter of fact, the more you discover how really fallible human beings are. Absolutely."

85

Esquire: "But you don't let it bug you?"

Hefner: "It does sometimes, but I don't let it bug me overall. I have no ulcers. I sleep like a baby."

That pretty much tells the story. What Hefner neglected to tell the *Esquire* interviewer was that what saves the top executives who make mistakes is their utter loyalty to Playboy and "Hef." This realization stirred my resentment, bringing the rebellion in me closer to the surface. It was at that point I began calling Hefner "Huf" instead of the endearing "Hef" used by his loyal followers and close friends.

I eventually came to believe that no matter how much pruning was done at the middle-management level, giving the company the vitality it needed was going to be difficult—if not impossible.

Once in a meeting with Hefner, Preuss and Rosenzweig, a serious disagreement between Hefner and myself arose. It clearly showed me what I was up against. Preuss said, "Well, I see points to what both of you are saying but I suppose I would have to go along with Hef on it." And Rosenzweig—who, two hours earlier, had agreed with me on the issue involved—now replied, "Well, I just don't know, I'd prefer not to cast a vote."

After the meeting I said, "Dick, why didn't you say what you did to me before the meeting? How could you sit there and say nothing?"

"Well, I feel that my role is to explain to Hefner anything he doesn't understand and to attempt to help him formulate his views," he told me.

"Do you honestly mean," I said, "that if you feel he is doing something absolutely wrong, you will let him do it improperly because it isn't your role to help convince him?"

"Yes," he said, "I suppose that's what I'm saying."

After that meeting I didn't ask Preuss why he didn't express his views. But on other occasions I did, and he'd say, "Look, the time wasn't right," or "I want to get Hefner alone on that subject," or "It ought to be with so-and-so also there" or "If Spectorsky were there it would be much easier to accomplish it."

There was always some reason why the time was not ripe for Preuss and this was one of the great surprises to me—what an absolute pussycat he turned into around Hefner. When Preuss was conducting a meeting and Hefner wasn't there, Preuss was strong and assertive. He put down anyone whose views he disagreed with and then again, with an underling, sometimes he'd back down and say, "Well, look, why don't you think about this different approach and I'm sure you'll see it my way."

(It was Preuss, in fact, who taught me how to ask questions. He was a master at asking questions about questions—that is, questioning the premises. If, for example, someone says X is blue and Y is red, therefore Z is purple, most people would question whether the answer was Z. Few people would ask, "How do you know X is blue and Y is red?" And that's the key to successful negotiating and successful business in general. People are rarely certain of their accepted premises in business.

(Preuss taught me well. The first time we met, he had the upper hand. The second time he still had the upper hand. The third time we were equal. And from then on, I always had the upper hand at our meetings. This approach, of course, is not always a winning one. You may still lose your argument. But if nothing else, you at least throw your opponent off guard.)

I recognized Preuss' weakness in facing up to Hefner the day of the foreign editions meeting when I saw him sitting there, head down, doodling. I noticed after that that he did very extensive doodles any time we were in a meeting with Hefner. Once I started to analyze one of them and that upset Preuss. After Hefner left, I looked at Preuss' doodle and in front of several of the others I said, "Bob, look at what you've done here, see how tight it is, how constricted, it means that you're really uptight. What's going on?"

He was too furious to answer.

Preuss and I frequently talked about the yes-man approach, but he didn't look at it as yes-man. He saw it as no one having the capability to challenge Hefner. The reason he

87

had never done so, he said once, was because he had never had sufficient support. He did now, I assured him. I couldn't wait until the next meeting Preuss and I would both attend.

I didn't have to wait long. Shortly after my conversation with Preuss another meeting was set up at the Mansion. And—Preuss sat there doodling on his pad, not saying a word.

Chapter 8
A Free Enterprise System

If ever there was a time when coming events should have cast their shadows before, it was the night I skulked through the dark corridors of Playboy, intent on thievery.

Talk about getting caught with your pants down!

What led to my embarrassment was simple enough: One of my co-workers—a pretty high-ranking executive—had refused to give me access to a confidential report that had already been widely circulated. This was before I became marketing director, so I did not have the clout to request and immediately get such a report.

But dammit, that refusal was a blow to my ego, my professional pride, my self-respect, and perhaps more important—my trustworthiness. It also served to reinforce that particular executive's status in the pecking order. What a put-down. I was left with only one course of action: to steal the report.

The waiting game began one Friday evening. My strategy was simple enough. I would stay until 6:30, a safe time since everyone usually left by 5 sharp, and then strike. In fact,

Playboy at 5 p.m. always reminded me of the pop slogan that apathetically states: "Tomorrow has been cancelled due to lack of interest." Finally, zero hour came.

I took the elevator to the executive's floor. (Even if the place were pitch dark I knew I would have no trouble making my way to his office because all ten floors comprising the Playboy offices have basically the same floor pattern.) The lights were all out. Slowly and silently I crept past the reception area, making my way along the sand-finished sculptured wall of the corridor that led to the office area, where during the day the drone from the electric typewriters of the secretarial pool could be heard. Now the silence was deafening. Even my footsteps were muffled by the lush carpeting.

My pace quickened as I reached the area and focused my eyes on his closed office door. There was no trace of light from under it. I was home free if it wasn't locked. I turned the knob, opened the door and bolted in, all in one sweeping motion.

What I saw was like a scene out of a Henry Miller novel: This executive's secretary was sitting in his chair vigorously exercising her oral capacities as he stood before her. To say she had a mouthful was an understatement. She was giving him a "blow-job."

Then—splash! At the sound of my entrance he had jerked around toward me, startled, and before I could say "excuse . . . " he had ejaculated all over my suit.

"Omigod, I'm - I'm terribly sorry," he stammered. "Let me pay for the cleaning."

I looked down at the semen dripping over the front of the jacket and trousers of my dark blue worsted suit. And then I looked at him standing there with his penis hanging out of his trousers and said:

"Pardon me, can you tell me where the nearest john is?" I didn't wait for an answer.

I abruptly walked out, closing the door, and stopped in the men's room just long enough to clean off my suit. I couldn't get out of that place fast enough.

From then on, I was ready to expect anything I might

experience in the Playboy domain. Also from then on, I had only to walk within sight of the executive and he turned a bright red. For the remainder of my stay at Playboy he never looked me in the eye when he spoke to me. Nor did he ever ask me why I had entered his office that infamous evening. And I never pressed him for the cleaning bill, either. As for the secretary—an efficient one at that—he let her go shortly thereafter, to the bewilderment of her co-workers. Only the three of us, of course, knew why.

Incidentally, to this day I treat that blue suit as if it were something from a leper colony. It hangs forlornly in my closet as a constant reminder of my unconventional baptism in sex at Playboy.

It was an unsavory event, proving to me that free enterprise is not dead at Playboy. Other activities involved instances of hanky-panky, homosexuality, divorce and drugs, not to mention the clothes freaks.

None of them are new. And like the pecking order, they exist in all corporations, in all strata of society. It's the extent that astounded me.

Take, for example, the area of divorce. Between 60 and 80 percent of the people I came in contact with at Playboy had been divorced at least once. Hefner, divorced once; Spectorsky, divorced twice; Rogers, three times; Rosenzweig, Morton, Lownes and Robert Gutwillig (vice president of publishing development) were all divorced. And that's just the upper echelon. At least eight middle-management people in the promotion department were legally split.

I am uncertain why the incidence was so high. Many, of course, were divorced before they joined Playboy. Perhaps divorcees seek Playboy as a refuge of sorts, lured by the fantasy of a free-swinging organization that promises untold sexual adventures. The divorce ratio is, however, the broader manifestation that at Playboy people fool around for serious.

Perhaps it was that oral sex incident that jolted my psyche into becoming more sensitive to the hanky-panky around me. Up to that point I had been totally oblivious to the fun and games that were going on. I never did go in for locker room gossip about who was screwing whom. But somehow I couldn't help myself. Suddenly the secretaries and their bosses became suspect in my mind's eye, reduced to the scene I had burst in on that night.

I had to continually remind myself that promiscuity at Playboy was no different than at any other big corporation. And I couldn't convince myself that it was less flagrant anywhere else. After all, what organization employing 4,000 red-blooded men and women (900 are Playboy Bunnies) wouldn't have its problems? The CIA, maybe?

I would say the swinging atmosphere prevailing at Playboy is somewhere on the high side of whoopee. Friends and associates outside the company often asked me just how wild the Playboy secretaries really were. The question was asked so often that I was compelled to find an answer. So, in the line of research, I began to observe the secretaries with a more critical eye.

Playboy takes great pride in its secretaries. They are all young and pleasant-looking. In fact, youth and good looks are job requisites, just as important as secretarial skills. Playboy's open dress code gives them a great deal of latitude to make themselves very alluring.

Some of the secretaries have done quite well for themselves. One of Hefner's favorites in the early 1960s was a blond Chicagoan named Cynthia Maddox. At nights she was a Playboy Bunny and during the day a Playboy secretary. Hefner, however, never could persuade Cynthia to pose for the centerfold. When I was at Playboy Claudia Jennings was discovered or rather uncovered as a Playboy receptionist to become the November 1969 Playmate. She went on to become the 1970 Playmate of The Year and her career has since progressed into cinema and stage roles. The Playboy offices are packed with secretaries just waiting to be discovered. But until they are, it's open season on secretaries at Playboy.

I really didn't give a damn about the office romancing unless it affected the functioning of the office. And sometimes it did just that. For a while things were pretty quiet. So much so, that I began to think the scene I barged in on was a totally isolated situation. Then one morning I heard a shrill cry outside my office as a secretary, jilted by her lover, made a delirious dash down the corridor incoherently warbling the name of her lost love—a Playboy executive.

Then there was a dapper fellow in the public relations department who had trouble maintaining his authority because he was shacking up with a busty secretary of one of his staffers. Another secretary became involved with a young writer in editorial. He was a relatively unscrupulous guy, who was also pumping her for salary and other confidential information she was privy to. He would then spread the information around the company, causing dissension among the more competitive-minded personnel. But it was one of the affairs in my department that finally got to me. A fellow in the promotion department was shacking up with one of Hefner's secretaries. Normally, it wouldn't have made any difference to me, but in this instance it did. I started getting feedback from other department personnel on portions of memos that had been written by Hefner for Preuss and myself. The memos dealt with the company's direct mail order advertising efforts and were not that secret. But I knew that forthcoming memos would be more important and those were the ones I was worried about. I traced the leak to the source and I fired him. It was either that or break up a romance and that definitely was not part of my job.

About a week later I almost did an encore of my earlier performance when I broke in on the executive and his secretary. This time, however, it was a solo situation rather than a duet. I had been looking for several hours for one of my associates, leaving word with his secretary to contact me upon his return. While on the phone I noticed him sauntering past my office with a large box tucked under his arm. Before I could get his attention he entered his office, closing the door behind him. It was an unusual gesture because he had always worked with his door opened. I was sure his secretary had given him my message, emphasizing its urgency. But there was no response. I walked to his office and tapped gently on the door. There was no response. My immediate thought was that he was napping, or totally immersed in his work. There were times when my concentration made me oblivious to what was going on around me. His secretary had left her desk for a coffee break so I had to forego the courtesy of being announced. I opened the door only to find my hunch confirmed. He was concentrating—but not on business.

Scattered over his desk were stacks of untouched photographic transparencies of various Playmates in poses too base or seductive for the centerfold spread.

"Oh, hi, Steve, I didn't hear you knock," he said, flashing a grin. In one hand he was holding a transparency. His other hand was in his pocket gripping his crotch.

"What are you doing with those transparencies?" I asked, hoping the answer would be a logical one. This executive had absolutely nothing to do with the Playmates or the promotion of the Playmates that would require him to review such transparencies.

"A friend of mine from editorial let me borrow them. They're damn good shots," he said. By now his grin had become a grimace and he had flushed to his ears. His nonchalant air had changed into the awkward embarrassment of a kid whose mother had caught him masturbating. Only, this was no kid—at least not chronologically.

"I would just like to know two things," I said, "why the hell don't you lock your damn door if you want privacy and didn't you get my message?"

"I didn't lock my door because I had no idea I would become so engrossed in the transparencies. And I intended to call you back within the hour."

"Well, when you're finished doing whatever you have to do, I'd like to go over some ads with you in my office," I said, slamming the door behind me.

These were all private or inside incidents, so to speak. But I soon found out that inside or outside made no difference to some Playboy executives.

One day, for example, I was driving down Michigan Avenue and I saw a Playboy associate with a beautiful brunette, kissing her in public. I had met his wife and that wasn't her.

Another day I was in a taxi passing the Ambassador Hotel and there, arm-in-arm, was another associate with his chief's secretary.

Once I was walking into the Playboy Building and I saw another cohort walking out hand-in-hand with a girl. I said to myself, from what I know about his wife, she's not it. I assumed that because I had a copy of his audit—his shrink report—and when he talked about his wife he got across the idea that he didn't like her, that she was a cold fish. And here he was with this vibrant, vivacious girl. As I walked by I said hello and he said, "Hi, Steve," and started to walk a little faster. I said, "Hey, introduce me to your wife," and he answered, "This isn't my wife, just an old friend." The two of them walked out of the lobby, still hand-in-hand.

That was the kind of thing that went on and often it was serious enough to lead to the divorce courts and up the divorce percentage at Playboy.

But it might have been higher if the wives they left behind had seen their husbands in Las Vegas.

This was an amazing thing. It gave me an insight into human nature. It showed me that some people are so unconcerned with their self-image and the image of themselves in the eyes of others that they are willing to degrade themselves in return for the most basic pursuit of pleasure.

Anyone would think that at least some of the advertising salesmen of Playboy would cover their actions but it didn't happen in Vegas. These fellows were the source of heavy revenue for the hookers hanging out in the lobbies of the hotels.

The busy, open hustling of the hookers and bargaining down of the prices and the deal-making was whoremongering that rivaled what goes on every night at 42nd Street and Broadway in New York. It made me wonder if they were as conscientious in their business negotiations.

One evening I was sitting at a table with three of the ad salesmen discussing airline advertising when a blonde hooker started a conversation with one of them she had met earlier in the day. They settled on $25 as the fee and that was the last we saw of him that evening.

The following evening I stopped at a blackjack table and was losing a few dollars when this hooker sat down beside me and said, "Hey, that little friend of yours . . . " and I said, "Lady, he's no friend of mine, he's merely an associate." She said, "Well, he sure has strange tastes." I asked her what she meant and she said, "I'm talking about the whips and chains he was looking for but couldn't find in his room. He had to settle for hitting me with his shoe."

"Don't you mind being hit with a shoe?" I asked. She paused and thoughtfully replied, "Well, I really sort of enjoyed it." Come to think of it, after whips and chains, a shoe she'd hardly feel.

Another Las Vegas incident made me wish I carried a movie camera. One of the executives who was supposed to be there to tell the advertising sales force how to improve its efforts had the gall to bring his girl friend, who was a Playboy research assistant. He skipped most of the meetings to be with her.

One evening Preuss, two other associates and I were walking from the Sahara to the Stardust and all of a sudden we saw this fellow and the girl but he hadn't seen us yet. When he did he gave the girl a shove that sent her almost reeling and he himself took three steps backward. If this was meant to fool anybody, it didn't. As we passed him, we spoke to him and he just walked along with his head up as if he didn't either hear or see us. His blundering in public was typical of the kind of blunders he was making in his job. Three days after we got back from Las Vegas, I fired him. That incident only served to remind me how really inept he was.

Now, as I said, in addition to incidents of divorce and hanky-panky there were instances of homosexuality, everything from innuendoes and little hints thrown out to grab-ass and things like that. Jay Rosenberg and Marty Bass and I were in a meeting once with two of them (one is no longer with Playboy, one is) and Rosenberg was sitting on a sofa with one on each side.

The more obvious of the two edged over until his arm was on the back of the sofa above Rosenberg's head and then he just casually dropped his hand down on Rosenberg's shoulder. He'd done this bit by bit and Rosenberg looked up and said, "Please don't touch me, I'm terribly strange about that."

There's this one guy—he must be one of the great queers of the Western world, oh, such a queer. One time I saw him at Playboy's annual fashion affair at the Plaza Hotel in New York and he called to me.

"Stephen, Stephen," he said as I walked toward him. "Come here, my dear boy." Then he turned and said, "Mother, I want you to meet Stephen Byer, this dear young man I've told you about."

I wanted to say I have a wife and two children. But instead I said how do you do. She said it, too—in a very deep, throaty voice. She has short hair, much shorter than mine, and she's masculine-looking. In that very deep voice she asked her son to get her a drink and in a very high voice he said, "Yes, mother," and there's a voice reversal, if nothing else. I quickly excused myself, I didn't want any part of that.

(I can't help wondering if there is a chapter about Playboy in the recently published book by Playboy Press entitled *Sex In The Executive Suite*. If there is, it should be highly entertaining.)

Even the way people dressed was somehow symptomatic of the general malaise around Playboy. For instance, Preuss wore fluorescent suits with tight pants. His jackets were nipped in at the waist and had cowboy pockets and a belt in the back. He was a faddist, but not in trim or style. If the fad for the week were purple jackets and fuchsia trousers with lemon yellow shirts and lime green ties, all done in Day-Glo felt, that was what he wore. He'd really get uptight when I kidded him about the fabric of his suit or the color or style.

Then, he would retaliate the next time I'd go to his office. He'd look me over and with a smirk he'd say, "Look at that tie, look at that—oh, Jesus, Connie (his secretary), come in here, would you, look at his tie—" He'd then go through this long shtick with his secretary about some article of my clothing.

Rogers was known for being a classic Madison Avenue type of dresser, but the sharpest dressers were Rosenzweig and Morton. Most people did not think Morton was, but I did because he dressed in more of a masculine, down-to-earth way. Everything was always nicely coordinated. Arnold dressed the way I think I would if I paid a little more attention to it.

Rosenzweig really dresses like out of a fashion magazine, *Gentleman's Quarterly* or the fashion pages of *Playboy*. He's such a great dresser he's a dandy, he's a fop. Who wears a velvet suit?

Why, you can be attending the funeral of God with Rosenzweig, and as you're walking into the cemetery Dick will turn to you with his head bowed and say, "Where'd you get the shirt?" Seriously, he and I were in some quite important meetings together and I'd say, "Dick, what do you think of what they have to say?" and he'd say, "Pretty good, pretty good, where'd you get that shirt?" He's a shirt freak.

Hefner—what can you say about yellow pajamas and an orange bathrobe? When he did wear clothing-type clothing he was always a year behind the style. Hefner wearing Edwardian suits, Hefner wearing narrow jackets or Apache scarves—always out of vogue approximately a year to fifteen months. Hefner always looks like he has just come back from some tailor who's foisted off on him stuff that other people have returned for credit against their next suit.

But he takes his out-in-public clothing very seriously, he's over-conscious of his appearance. This is perhaps contradicted by the way he conducts meetings, dressed in that robe and pajamas. But that, I think, is a statement to the effect that I, Hugh Hefner, don't have to dress for these common laborers who work for me. But when he is going out in public he is hyper-conscious of the way he looks. I have seen him getting ready to appear in public and he's like a little old lady primping and pampering before the mirror.

(Hefner, in fact, was so conscious of his public image he would blow his stack whenever he saw a photograph of himself that he didn't like. I remember his reaction to one particular photograph that showed him debarking from the Big Bunny on his arrival in Morocco as part of an intercontinental tour he took in 1970. Clutching the photograph in his hand, he ranted: "I don't believe it, I don't believe it. Why did he [the photographer] shoot that? Why did he develop it?" Hefner was absolutely livid. I had never seen him that way before.

(I must admit that the picture didn't do him justice. I suppose it was a tiring trip because the expression on his face made him look like he had just passed the basket-weaving test at the institution where he was being maintained as a vegetable. And there was Barbi—who didn't help the picture any—looking up at him with a vacant, distant look on her face.)

Robert Gutwillig, about 41, dresses in a studied affectation of a New York journalist. He wears deerskin moccasins—the kind you wear as house slippers—with leather-elbowed tweed jackets and a tie purposely askew and always has that look of "Oh, God, I'm so haggard." Well, I suppose he had the right to dress that way, considering his experience in the publishing field. He had been editorial vice president of World Publishing Company, and had held a similar position with New American Library. He had also been employed as executive editor of the Trade Book Department of McGraw-Hill Publishing Company. He joined Playboy as vice president, publishing development, in January 1970. A graduate of Cornell University, Gutwillig's roommate there at one time was author Clifford Irving, whose alleged autobiography of Howard Hughes—branded as a hoax—jolted the world.

Victor A. Lownes III dresses quite well, a little overdone for my taste, but he wears clothes well and in contemporary styles.

Hefner's father, Glenn, vice president and treasurer of HMH Publishing, also has his own style of dress. What can you say about seersucker suits and half-inch-wide ties?

Glenn is not very verbal. He reminds me of a cardboard cutout, with a little voice box mechanism inside, that smiles and says: "Hello, I'm Glenn Hefner, Hugh's da-da."

After about ten months at Playboy I thought it was time I met him, so I phoned and said, "Glenn, this is Steve Byer, I would like to meet you after all this time. May I come up to your office?" And he said, "Yes."

"Well, Glenn," I said as I sat down, "how are you today?"

The conversation pretty much ended right there; he just mumbled.

"Glenn," I tried again, "you certainly have a lovely view."

More mumbles.

"Glenn," and I was getting desperate, "is there anything I can tell you about my operation that would be helpful for you to know?"

More mumbles.

Well, I stuck it out for about ten minutes and then I gave up, I was so uncomfortable, so tongue-tied, it was like talking to yourself—no, it was worse than talking to yourself.

Glenn Hefner is 76 so I guess he has a right to mumble if he wants to. There is no mandatory retirement age at Playboy. Glenn is paid $41,000 a year.

Hefner's brother, Keith, about 40, left Playboy a few years ago and now runs a leather goods shop somewhere in Colorado.

The use of drugs by people at Playboy included smoking pot. Parts of the building frequently reeked. Some were on hard drugs, too. Of two Playmates I knew about, one was taken out of all promotional appearances because she was a heroin addict.

And when one of the promotion staff left Playboy he was given a large container of peyote and mescaline as a going away present from the rest of the staff. Another of the promotion people was a drug addict and so badly affected by it that he's living on Skid Row in Los Angeles.

If I hadn't stopped smoking entirely about four years ago, my natural curiosity probably would have led me to at least

100

try pot, but I didn't, because I was determined not to smoke ever again.

At one time one of my secretaries began to use drugs extensively, LSD, peyote and mescaline. Before I discovered that, I thought she was getting to be a little on the crazy side, or just freaking out intellectually. I had to fire her. Another one of my staffers was an example of a middle-aged man discovering pot. He'd sit around saying things like, "Oy, I'm getting high."

And there was a drug-induced episode in Los Angeles that was kept out of the newspapers. One of the Bunnies was so badly beaten by her one-time boyfriend that she was hospitalized for two or three weeks. Both of them were on LSD.

The drug-taking didn't really bother me unless I had to work with someone under the influence. One I remember—his drug was alcohol. Day in and day out, he came back from a three-hour "lunch" and he was loaded. And he stayed loaded for the rest of the afternoon. He has been at Playboy thirteen years, he is a hard-core lush, and he is an example of the worst sort of deadwood that exists there.

All these things were easy to accept and really never bothered me. But there was one general practice that did. Spying!

Chapter 9
Tom, Dick and (Mata) Hari

Spying at Playboy is deep, entrenched, a part of everybody's life. Everyone spies on everyone else, reports to someone about someone else, and they are all insecure because of this spying, even though they themselves are participating.

Every conversation, every happenstance, every private thing is repeated and frequently is brought back to the person under scrutiny with an accusatory finger being pointed at him or her, demanding why did this happen, how did it happen, is it true this happened, explain yourself.

I caught on the first week when Preuss called me in and questioned me on why I told Bud Bruder—the land development guy—that he was incapable of handling Playboy products.

"After all," Preuss said, "is this any way to ingratiate yourself among your fellow executives, when you've just joined the company?"

Now, what had really happened is that Bud Bruder remarked to me, "Hell, I don't know anything about this," and I said, "In that case, and since this is my area of specialization, why don't we take it off your hands?" He agreed. But it had been played back to Preuss that I just walked into Bud's office and said, "Bud, you don't know anything about Playboy products, I'm taking over, like it or not."

That was when I began to become cautious. And as other incidents began to unfold, I eventually even started locking my office when I left.

The John Mastro episode was one. Mastro was head of the production department and one day when I was working on an ad series he called me and said, "You have a September 1 due date for proofs. This is already August 23, so if you want them by the first it's going to cost us a few dollars more."

"Ok, fine, John," I told him, "then let's do it, because I've promised Hefner that I'd have the ads ready for him to look at in proof form by that date. I have a meeting with him that afternoon."

As the day drew near, Hefner cancelled the meeting because he was going out of town. Between when the meeting was to have taken place and when it did, Preuss called me in and said, "You have authorized the expenditure of $1,500 for rush proofs for a meeting that isn't scheduled."

He told me Mastro reported to him that I demanded proofs by September 1, at an overtime charge of $1,500, and that Mastro happened to ask my secretary if I was meeting with Hefner on that day and she said no.

"You tell John Mastro," I said, "that number one, he said it would be a 'few' dollars more, and number two, when or if I have my meetings with Hefner is none of his business. And furthermore, for your information, Hefner cancelled the September 1 meeting and changed it to September 8."

Another Preuss example: One day he said to me, "I have it on good word that one of your men"—meaning one of the people I had brought to Playboy—"refers to me as a greasy Polack and I resent it very much. I will not tolerate being referred to that way by an underling. It's ok if you and I kid each other about being a Polack or something like that, but I won't take it from some underling."

I asked whom he meant and he said, "I'm talking about

Rosenberg." And I said, "A greasy Polack? I've never heard Rosenberg refer to you in other than a fairly respectful manner. I say fairly respectful because there are some questions in his mind as to some of your judgments about his activities and if I were you I'd look at the fairly respectful manner and count my blessings."

"Don't get smart about it," he retorted, "I don't want this little bastard referring to me as a greasy Polack again. Just tell him to knock it off."

When I talked to Jay about it, he was shocked.

Another time, Al Teller, the corporate development director, told me Preuss had accused him of looking for a new job, basing his charge on "very good information." He told Al that if he continued to do it on Playboy's time, he then would have to find one.

"You mean he was really serious about it?" I asked Al. He said absolutely, that Preuss chewed him out, saying he had it from a source he would not name that on or about September 1, 1970, Alvin M. Teller had been interviewing for a new job with a company in Chicago.

Of course, it wasn't true, just another spy job, another false rumor relayed to Preuss.

But Preuss wasn't the only one on the spy network. The head of the telephone service, a gal no longer with Playboy, once told me that part of her job was to meet the phone company representative once a month and check out all the long distance calls that took place after 5:30 on the company's wire. This was done not to cut down on the telephone bill but to try to determine why people were making long distance calls after 5:30.

I'm sure that was the motive because I was asked to verify literally hundreds of telephone calls that people on my staff made. I was told how these things were checked out. For example, a call would be made to a company with a small switchboard, saying they were just investigating the telephone bill and to whom at that number would a call from someone at Playboy have gone? Then they would try to find out the relationship.

Besides this corporate spying, there were plants. At one point, another vice president decided that he needed more knowledge of promotional activities surrounding the entertainment division. He suggested to his then-assistant that she ask me if she couldn't be transferred to the promotion department or to my immediate staff.

She first asked if she could become my administrative assistant and I told her I was against such categorical functions because I felt they reeked of empire building. So then she asked if she could go to work in the promotion department (my ears pricked up because I knew she hated Futch, the promotion manager) but perhaps report to me in most capacities?

I told her no, she couldn't report to me, but if Futch needed her or could use her, she could work there. Well, she was able to replace someone who was leaving. Three months later I had gotten to know her pretty well because her office was near mine and she'd come in and we'd chat for a little while.

One day she came in, closed the door, sat down and said, "I have something to tell you and I think you will be perfectly justified in firing me, but I want to tell you because I very much respect the job you've done here. I feel like a real traitor because my boss set up my going to work for the promotion department so I could report back to him all of the details about the department and specifically how it was working on entertainment division projects. He didn't feel that he would get a straight answer from Futch and you."

"In other words," I said, "you came here as a spy?" She said yes, and started to cry, so I said, "Hey, that's ok, I'm glad you told me. It gives me a better impression of your character than I've had until now, because I've known this all along."

She said I couldn't have known. I told her it was obvious, when she suddenly said she wanted to work for me, that there couldn't have been any other reason. After all, I knew her boss and how his mind worked.

She asked if I wanted her to leave and I said no, of course

not, she was doing a good job, I just wanted her not to report to her former boss anything other than she would ordinarily report to any operational head she was serving. In her capacity as media promotion manager she had access to records and dealt with all of the segments or divisions of the company.

Executives' secretaries—well, one was instructed to act as a spy whenever she could. She asked seemingly harmless questions of other secretaries, chatting about one thing and another, but taking specific directions, like why is so-and-so in . . . what are we doing with that company or this person . . . is it true that so-and-so is interviewing people for a position . . . things like that.

It was so obvious that the girls laughed about it behind her back and certainly fed her wrong information.

And the Bunnies. The Bunnies were spied upon by the widest variety of people. Bunny mothers, the club managers, the assistant managers, the night managers, the Playboy Clubs International operational people who would periodically frequent the clubs, and people sent in by the PCI operational people to try and strike up an acquaintance with the Bunnies.

I guess like was treated with like here, because despite all these deceitful practices, all this spying, the Bunnies were doing anything they wanted to, anyway.

Now, there was an incident concerning Jay Rosenberg, Nelson Futch and his secretary, and what was then Byer-InterMark Corp.

My present company, Byer/InterMark, Inc., is an off-shoot of a company I formed while I was working for Playboy. It was incorporated in March 1970 and Hefner knew all about it and had given me his permission to form it. I told him I wished to form a personal service corporation to pursue certain outside interests and that it was nothing that would take me away from my responsibilities to Playboy.

So one day after I had left Playboy Enterprises, Rosenberg was walking by the Xerox machine and he saw Futch huddled over it with his secretary, and Nelson sort of leaned over to shield what he was copying more closely. On the way back, just on a wild hunch—Jay lifted up the cover where the original is placed and there it was. They'd forgotten it. He grabbed it, stuffed it in his pocket, went to his office and looked at it. It was a Dun and Bradstreet report on Byer-InterMark and it stated who the stockholders were. Jay was one, so was Marty Bass.

The following day, Jay and Marty complained that every time they made a telephone call there was a clicking on the line that had never occurred before, and that it was harder to hear.

Of course, I didn't know all these things when I started locking my door. I have a funny habit, I remember precise positions of certain things. When I leave my office in the evening I make a mental note of the fact that the tape recorder is slanted on the desk a certain way, or that my calendar book is lined up flush with the edge of the desk, and other things like that.

Well, I'd noticed at times that things were misaligned or their position altered, and this was not attributable to either my secretary or the cleaning women. The cleaning women never touched anything on the conference tables but I'd find stacks of papers awry, for example.

But what I'd also noticed was that two fellows were always at the office, one or the other of them, on the occasions when I left and then found things disturbed the next day. So, short of lurking in the corridor and risking being spotted, I decided instead to lock my office even if it meant it wasn't cleaned.

There were other examples. One day one of my men told me that his files had been ransacked and that a number of documents were missing. The following day another reported missing files. My filing cabinets had locks on them, theirs did not. And about a month later Lance Hooper mentioned a Playboy Preferred situation and I realized who had taken those files.

I went to Preuss and said, "You have this guy working for you next door and I want to tell you something. If I ever hear again of his removing things from the files of any of my

107

staff, I will physically kick the shit out of him." He said Lance wouldn't take someone else's file, but when I explained the situation he said, "Oh, that." So he knew about it.

"Well, let me tell you why," he said. "Don't go feeling antagonistic toward Lance, he was doing it for all of our best interests. There's some conversation that maybe some of the personnel are taking some kickback on our direct mail merchandising efforts."

"You must be out of your mind," I told him, "I've known them for years and there is no way they could be taking a kickback unless I am, and you know I'm not." But Preuss couldn't understand the concept of personal loyalty.

So there was that sort of spying at Playboy, too, slanderous in nature.

And let's don't forget the personnel department that Theo Frederick runs. It is a micro-type police state, a little secret police operation. Calls are made to secretaries by the personnel department secretaries asking questions about their bosses, surreptitious questions like, I heard your boss does so and so, questions about his personal habits, or his family, or his hours, all asked in an offhand manner but clearly forming a pattern of the personnel department's secretaries being used as little agents.

Last, but very far from least, is the rumor mill. It is phenomenal. Someone is fired, it's all over the building in 15 minutes. Someone is hired, everyone knows about it. Some guy gets his ass chewed by Hefner, everyone hears it. Hefner sends a scathing memo on some project, not only does everybody know about it but copies spread through the building.

It is as if no one has any other concern than relating the day's crap to somebody else.

Chapter 10
All In The Family

You can divide the people at Playboy into three groups, the malcontents, the ones that can take it or leave it, and the ones that think it's great.

Over the years the news media has consistently lauded the camaraderie in the Hefner organization, the one big happy family idea. That's so far from the feeling in that corporation it's like chicken salad and chicken shit.

Executive magazine, in its June 1968 issue, said that "perhaps the most constructive aspect of Playboy is the enthusiasm and confidence which permeates every level of the organization, from Hefner down to the secretaries, whose laughter punctuates recordings of interviews with chief executives."

If that reporter found camaraderie in 1968 it must have deteriorated fast because I found a decidedly different atmosphere in 1969 in regard to the all pals together concept as well as *Executive's* "enthusiasm and confidence."

One middle-management fellow never stopped bitching

about Playboy. "If I had any guts," he'd say, "I'd find another job." A copywriter forced Playboy to fire him by simply not showing up for three weeks straight because he couldn't take any more of such a messed-up organization.

An executive who has been with the company more than ten years is the first to wax negative about Playboy, not only in private but at public gatherings. I once said to him, "If I hear another negative tirade about Playboy before outside people you're going to be out of a job." I was astounded once by his saying, "Well, of course we're going to do it right, we're going to do it the way the master wants it done, and whatever that comes to, that'll be right." That's the kind of thing he said to people from advertising agencies.

A really big wheel at Playboy cannot stand the organization. He feels that it stopped being positive and progressive when he was transferred out of headquarters, when he was forced out by Hefner, a move that was instituted by Preuss.

The head of one department has been looking for another job for maybe three or four years. Two of his staff are so discontented they're constantly quitting and then thinking it over, but they're always on the lookout for jobs.

The head of another department was fired while I was there because of his bad attitude, so obviously he was a malcontent. Turnover in his area is constant.

They kept one good man as long as they did, obviously, only by paying him the exorbitant amount he wanted. The girl one of my own executives sent to spy on me resigned shortly after I left. The office next to hers was occupied by a fellow I fired because his attitude was so negative. One executive assistant has never had a positive thing to say about Playboy other than that he's gotten his Christmas bonus every year.

The traffic girls. One night one of them typed a memo and had it copied and distributed to everyone in the company: "I've been with this organization for seven years. You can keep my profit-sharing, I don't even want it anymore. I'm leaving. Goodbye." And she left, just like that. Her assistant can take it or leave it.

A key manager, with the company about fifteen years now, has never stopped complaining about its nature, how bad it is, how he is the only one who knows his job. Ask him if he wants to stay and he'll say, "Sure, what the hell, I've been with this company for fifteen years." But talk about attitude—everyone he comes in contact with is an idiot, to hear him tell it.

Spectorsky felt that there was no one other than himself who was capable or competent. Mark Demarest? I didn't know exactly what Demarest felt. He was heading up the whole foreign edition project, so he'd escaped. But apparently he couldn't get far enough. He quit shortly after the foreign assignment.

Is all this camaraderie?

One of the assistant managing editors, a sharp, intelligent guy, stays only because he thinks present policies are so poor that there has to be a future for someone intelligent.

All this is enthusiasm, confidence, camaraderie?

What kind of attitude is it when Hefner writes a memo on women's lib and somebody steals it and distributes it to *Seed*, the Chicago underground newspaper, and anybody else who will take the damn thing?

And how did that memo to Preuss discussing *Essence* magazine get out of Gutwillig's confidential file? He had been detailed to safeguard the Playboy investment of $250,000 in the black woman's service magazine with the largest circulation—between 110,000 and 150,000—in the country. He was supposed to serve in an advisory capacity and had his instructions from Preuss. This supervision was approved by the Hollingsworth Group, Inc., publishers of *Essence*.

The leak of that memo was to have far-reaching results at *Essence*. On May 5, 1971, at a press conference in the Overseas Press Club in New York City, Jonathan Blount, the founder of *Essence*, charged that Playboy was making a "blatant" attempt to take over his magazine.

C. Gerald Fraser reported in an article printed in *The New York Times* on May 6 that Blount said that when he asked the board of directors to prevent the takeover, he was dis-

111

missed both as president and as a board member. With Blount at the conference were Ida Lewis, the recently dismissed editor-in-chief, and four top staff members who had resigned in sympathy.

Fraser wrote that the new president of the board, Clarence Smith, denied Blount's allegations and called them a "lot of nonsense."

But Blount said, according to Fraser: "Tangible evidence of Playboy's intentions came to my attention several months ago when I came into possession of a memo written by Bob Gutwillig, *Playboy* magazine's representative on the *Essence* board of directors. For exposing Gutwillig's memo, Playboy ordered my removal."

Blount distributed photocopies of the memo, which was written on stationery headed "Playboy. For Interoffice Correspondence."

The memo read in part:

"I am, of course, continuing to advise the *Essence* staff in the areas of my competence, and we continue effectively to dominate the board of directors with what now appears to be a solid coalition of five out of seven directors.

"In short, it looks as if we'll get a damn good run for our money."

Smith explained that Playboy's $250,000 was not in common stock but in preferred stock and five-year bonds. He said that Playboy's investment, if converted to common stock, would equal 10.8 percent of the total shares. At that time, 100 percent of the common stock was held by the men who raised the money and managed the magazine, the Hollingsworth Group. These were Blount; Ed Lewis, publisher; Cecil Hollingsworth, executive vice president, and himself.

Other investors included the Morgan Guaranty Trust Company, First National City Bank, Chase Manhattan and the John Hancock Life Insurance Company. Board members included the three Hollingsworth members and Russell Goings, all black, and Michael Victory and Gutwillig, white.

The *Times* quoted Lee Gottlieb, then vice president and director of public relations, as saying that the charges leveled

112

at Playboy were "absurd, as anyone who knows Playboy and its operation over the past years will attest. To comment further would only add importance to the accusations, which in no way merit such importance."

This camaraderie thing doesn't exist, it's imaginary.

Take Spectorsky and Rogers, who were certainly odd characters to find under the same corporate blanket, one having to convince himself of his own superiority by putting down everybody else, and the other finding his only security in agreeing with everybody's views.

Spectorsky must have been the unhappiest person in the world, if for no other reason than that he was not satisfied with another human being besides himself.

Among his major non-favorites were Art Paul and Vince Tajiri and even Hefner. He was two-faced with me, too. We'd end a conversation in perfect agreement and then later I'd get the drift back that he felt the advertising campaign, the media push, whatever we'd talked about, was absolutely terrible, when perhaps a day earlier he had said, "God, this is just fantastic."

But for a while after I left, three days never went by without Spectorsky asking me to have lunch with him. He would tell me such things as what a treacherous bastard this one associate of his was. And that he was trying to take over the editorial direction of the magazine behind Spectorsky's back.

He railed against Hefner and how Hefner had caused his heart attack because he would not allow him to do what he knew was best with the magazine, and how Hefner had turned over publishing development to Gutwillig and how this grated upon him so much. Then when Hefner decided to go into movie-making with "Macbeth" as the first venture, he did so against Spectorsky's recommendation and against mine and lot of other people's, too. Spec felt that director Roman Polanski had duped Hefner. It sent him into a wild rage.

"Hefner's gotten sucked into this," he'd say, "and it's sheer stupidity, it's folly, doesn't he know that Polanski's just trying to capitalize on Playboy, that he's going to lead us down the road and then leave us there and we're going to blow many millions on this?"

But his harshest and most vicious words were reserved for the Playboy clubs. Spectorsky said bitterly that he was earning money for the company through the magazine and Morton was kicking it away. The Los Angeles club had lost nearly a half-million dollars the preceding year, Spec argued, and why should Morton be allowed to piss away more money on new hotels when he couldn't run the old ones well enough?

Another top man he dubbed a silly old man, a brown shoes-white socks person who didn't represent the corporation properly; he was too conservative and the company should have a progressive man in that capacity.

He thought Art Paul was a power-hungry individual who resented Spectorsky's involvement in Playboy, and had rejected his authority from the first, saying, "Well, you're certainly no match for Hefner and that's who I'm used to dealing with."

Spectorsky told me that there was one period of two months when he didn't speak to Art because he was so displeased with him. Finally, Paul, wanting to make amends, wanting to dissolve the trauma, gave Spectorsky a present and as Spectorsky told me, "Do you know what he gave me? An autographed photograph of himself! Now, what kind of egotism or megalomania would cause a person to give someone an autographed photograph of himself as a gift?" I didn't know the answer to that.

I never asked Spectorsky why he stayed, feeling about his associates as he did, because all this venom didn't come out all at once. He'd bitch about one person or another and since it didn't all happen at one sitting, you'd think maybe there's a half-point there. But when you added them all up, what became clear was that this man never liked anyone. He never felt that anyone was capable, or that anyone was doing his job properly except himself.

But the truth is that Spectorsky had been the biggest rubber stamp editorial director of anyone within the entire

114

industry. Hefner to this day reads every page of every issue, reviews every transparency, photograph, print, illustration, article, and interview.

As for planning, Hefner again. Spectorsky submitted ideas to Hefner, but the final arbiter on everything editorially is Hefner. Hefner is going to do it the way he wants to do it.

Sure, Spectorsky held meetings with his own editorial staff, but all they did was to carry out Hefner's decisions. He never did control art and pictorial, because Art Paul never let Spectorsky dominate him. As time passed, Paul got more rather than less independent. Vince Tajiri, picture editor, was closer to Paul than to Spectorsky, so he didn't have any control over Tajiri either.

He did have control over his associate editors, Sheldon Wax, Murray Fisher, Nat Lehrman and Jack Kessie. Spectorsky only retained some control over the broadest aspects of the magazine, within the framework of what Hefner wanted.

Then there was Ted Rogers with his speech mannerisms. He gloms onto every phrase, every current catchword. Like when "right on" went from being a black power slogan to street slang, Rogers, upon hearing something that he wanted to indicate moved him, would say, "Right on, right on."

One of his greatest words is synergism, or synergistic or any variation of it. He was always talking about Playboy becoming a synergistic company and the need for synergism.

Other favorites were interface and hardware and software and programming, all the variations of that. "He's not programmed for that kind of software thinking," he'd say. And AV—audio-visual. "The day has to come when AV is everything," Rogers brought forth once, "and if this company ever shows any synergism, it'll bring itself to a point where the interface is so great that we're producing the software for the hardware people, right on."

There was one executive I began calling Mickey Mouse behind his back. It became so ingrained that if I had an appointment with him, I'd write it on my calendar, 1:30—Mouse. It became such a habit that whenever I'd get some paper or memo from him I'd automatically write "F/Mouse" on it for File/Mouse.

It was a habit I couldn't kick, and in the end it kicked me, in one of the last conversations I had with him.

We were involved in a big argument because he was doing something one way and I felt my way was more rational, so those two things worked against one another. I told him why— I would not do what he requested and he went into this long argument about why he was right and suddenly he started saying, "Now look, man, I don't go for that Mickey Mouse . . . "

This was after months of my referring to him as "Mouse," "Mick" or "Mickey." The first time he said that I wanted to smile but I pursed my lips tightly. The second time, 30 seconds later, I couldn't tighten my lips. The third time I started laughing hysterically, completely losing control. I doubled over and finally ran out of his office.

I couldn't help it, I was laughing so hard the tears were starting. As I was walking down the corridor, shrieking with laughter, I was thinking that does it, that guy will never speak to me again. I didn't mind that so much, but on the other hand, we both were employed by the same company.

An associate editor once wrote a memo to Spectorsky saying, "Spec, something's wrong here, something's wrong when you can roll a billiard ball down the corridors at 5 o'clock sharp and not hit a single person. There's something wrong when the editors take two-hour lunches when they should be working on a magazine that needs improvement."

He went on and on and all of his points were valid.

What was the response? Two weeks later he was fired. The memo firing him said that it was because he had "cheated on his expense accounts, had taken unauthorized trips, was trying to screw models and was cheating secretaries at bridge."

Were these the reasons? Or was it that memo two weeks earlier, with copies to no one, by the way, telling Spectorsky what was wrong at Playboy? I don't know, but . . .

Reverting to the camaraderie myth, there is no social

interrelationship among the various top executives at Playboy such as there is in virtually any other company. It's a distinct pattern, too distinct for there not to be a reason.

Hefner was never in my home because I didn't invite him. I don't believe he has been in Morton's home once, or ever in Preuss' or Rogers' or any of the others.

This is not to say that they're hostile out of the office but social mingling generally just does not occur. There were never any social functions that executives were required to attend. Playboy didn't believe in forcing its executives to be friends socially as do many big corporations.

Then there were the purely personal things. For instance, Lownes and I didn't contribute any camaraderie, either. For some reason, from the moment we met there was unbelievable friction between us. I guess it was what the shrinks call a personality clash. We had only to meet and we were arguing from word one.

The first time I met him at the Playboy building I said, "Vic, it's good to see you again," because I had met him briefly in 1960 at the club. And I went on, "You've taken off quite a lot of weight since I saw you last."

"I was never fat," he was glacial.

"I'm not saying you were fat but you do look good."

But he wouldn't unbend. "I have always looked good," he snapped.

It didn't bother me, because I knew why he was negative toward me. Years earlier Lownes had been known for being the same way I am. That is, he was known as a rough bastard and as the only guy to talk back to Hefner. But more than that, he had gotten a rundown on me and what I was doing to change things at Playboy and apparently he didn't like it. I had been given an authority he never had, and that triggered his negative attitude toward me. Naturally, I responded to what I instinctively felt was hostility. I never was one to turn the other cheek so there was never a chance of rapport between us.

Before I saw him that first time I thought that perhaps the years had mellowed him. But my next meeting with him

117

convinced me that they hadn't, not toward Byer, anyway.

We were in Morton's office discussing key sales and Lownes made a remark I disagreed with.

"Look, Vic," I said, "you're wrong," and I outlined it point by point. Lownes came back with some points of his own and I retorted, "That's irrational," and I went over it again, putting in some different aspects of the problem.

Lownes screamed at me in fury and what I now think was frustration, "Well, if you're so damn smart, how come I'm richer than you are?"

"Vic, you're right," I conceded, "you've got me, I can't think of an answer to that. But, at the very least, you're a bigger boor than I am."

After that Vic and I used different elevators.

Chapter 11
The Lone Stranger

If I had to describe Hugh Hefner in one word, I think I would choose his own, "loner." He has few intimate friends and no close family relationship. Despite his relatively recently donned public image of gregariousness and a flamboyant zest for the good life as he flits around the globe in his jet, he is still basically a recluse who has totally succumbed to the work ethic. He once described himself as a "loner kind of guy," who was a nonconformist with a cause. Playboy is that "cause" and nothing really distracts him from it, including fun, family and friends.

Hefner was the product of a strict, somewhat puritanical upbringing—"an earth fertile and ripe for the blossoming of a rebel," he once said. His parents, Glenn and Grace, were childhood sweethearts in Nebraska. They were married in the early 1920s and settled in Chicago, where Hugh and his brother, Keith, were born. "Ours was a strict Methodist household where there was no drinking or smoking, or even going to the show on Sunday. The moral discipline was strict but intellectual freedom was emphasized," Hefner told a

Chicago newspaper reporter who was once interviewing him.

His father, who had been a teacher in Nebraska, became a certified public accountant, work that took him away from home a great deal. Even as a young boy, Hefner showed a creative flair. He drew scores of cartoons, besides producing a "newspaper," which he sold at one cent per copy, detailing the activities of the boys in the neighborhood. The Hefners then lived in a modest apartment at 1922 N. New England Avenue on Chicago's West Side. Later, at Sayre Elementary School, Hugh founded a school paper called the *Pepper.* It was also during this period—the legend goes—that his I.Q. tested at a phenomenal 152. Hefner's high school days at Steinmetz were one of the happiest periods of his life, working on the *Steinmetz Star,* drawing cartoons and acting in school plays.

Upon graduation at 17, he joined the Army, serving in the infantry as a company clerk from 1944 to 1946. He also worked on educational and training programs and camp newspapers. After discharge, he attended the University of Illinois at Urbana with the help of the GI bill. He edited a humor magazine, *Shaft,* and contributed cartoons to the *Daily Illini.* He was graduated in 1949 with a major in psychology, earning his bachelor's degree in two and a half years.

His main reason for picking the University of Illinois was a girl named Millie Gunn and after graduation they were married. They had two children before their divorce in 1959. The children, a boy and a girl, live in Chicago with their mother, who has remarried. Hefner has not.

After graduation, Hefner took an apartment on Chicago's South Side at 6052 S. Harper Avenue. He tried to break into the publishing field but was forced to take a job with a firm that produced and printed cardboard cartons. Millie was teaching school. Hefner hated his job and decided to return to college to study for a master's degree in anticipation of becoming a teacher. After three months at Northwestern University he abandoned further study and got a $40-a-week job writing department store ad copy for Carson Pirie Scott

120

& Co. At night, he worked at his drawing board, producing a book of cartoons, "That Toddlin' Town," published in 1951.

Hefner found he was no happier writing ad copy than working for a carton manufacturer. When he heard of a job opening at *Esquire,* he managed to land it at $60 a week, but he was disappointed when he found his work lacked glamor and excitement.

In a letter written to a friend while working for *Esquire,* Hefner sketched his thoughts for a new magazine: "I'd like to produce an entertainment magazine for the city-bred guy— breezy and sophisticated. The girlie features would guarantee the initial sale but the magazine would have quality, too. Later, with some money in the bank, we'd begin increasing the quality and reducing the girlie features. We'd go after advertising and really make it an *Esquire*-type magazine."

When, in January 1952, *Esquire* moved its operation to New York, he was offered $80, asked for $85, was refused and quit. He then took an $80 job with Publisher's Development Corp., which put out a publication called *Children's Activities.* But as the months passed, Hefner's vision regarding editing his own magazine grew stronger. He talked about it in a 1961 *Chicago's American* (now called *Chicago Today*) series on Hefner: "I knew there must be others like me, urban in their interests, who wanted to read about sports cars and jazz and male fashions, who had a healthy interest in girls, who were looking for adult fiction and articles.

"I felt the years were going past and it would be harder to make the break in the future. So I talked to friends and friends of friends. I began selling stock."

He sold two kinds, 18,000 shares at a penny a share, all of which he kept himself for a half-interest in the company, and 18,000 shares at a dollar a share, of which he sold only $7,500 worth to 45 different investors. Hefner put up all the cash he could borrow from a bank—$600. And then he left his job to launch a magazine.

He got the "staff" to put out the first issue by offering stock instead of cash, as he did with Art Paul, a free-lance artist whose studio was in the Chicago Loop.

In November 1953 the first issue of *Playboy* came off the presses of a small printing plant in Rochelle, Illinois, a little town about 90 miles north of Chicago. It was a cold winter night and Hefner and his two associates (Art Paul and Eldon Sellers, an attorney), who helped him put the issue together, drove to Rochelle to watch their creation emerge. It was snowing while the three of them sat in a coffee shop across the street from the printer and made final corrections on the proof sheets.

That first issue of *Playboy* (Hefner wanted to call his magazine Stag Party but the publishers of a magazine with a similar name protested. It was Sellers who suggested Playboy) carried the legend Volume I, No. I, but no date because there was no guarantee there would ever be a second issue. Of the 70,000 copies printed, nearly 54,000 sold at 50 cents each at newsstands—an incredible number for a new magazine. Even Hefner was surprised by the initial success of his 48-page creation, which consisted of material mainly written by himself, except for the fiction. But he really shouldn't have been surprised, not with the secret weapon he unloaded—the nude calendar picture of Marilyn Monroe, then at the height of her career—and published in mass media for the first time. Hefner had purchased the reproduction rights for $200.

The second issue, bearing the date January 1954, was on the newsstands before Christmas. It carried Hefner's name on its title page as editor and publisher. The third issue carried Paul's name as art director, as has every issue since. The first three issues bore the return address of Hefner's apartment. But by the time the third issue was on the stands, Hefner had moved his operation to Chicago's Near North Side, renting the top floor at 11 East Superior Street.

Hefner picked a rabbit to symbolize his magazine because rabbits are the playboys of the animal world. In the first issue Hefner told readers that "we plan to spend most of our time inside. We like our apartment." What he didn't tell his readers, however, was that his indoor activities for the next fifteen years were going to be concentrated on working rather than playing. After all, dedicating one's self to a "cause" is serious business.

Hefner did not become a recluse until he moved into the Mansion in 1959 and from then until 1969 he stayed in his bedroom, sometimes for months on end, often working 36-hour shifts while subsisting on Pepsi-Colas and as many as 35 Dexedrine pills a day, in order to keep his "cause" going. It was a gaunt Hefner (40 pounds underweight) who stepped into the public light via newspaper and national magazine articles to denounce his self-exile and self-abuse. He was going to change his ways and begin practicing what he had been preaching all those years. He was going to play more and work less.

But why alert the public to Hefner's newly assumed facade? No one was clamoring for a new and reformed Hefner. No one, that is, except Playboy's public relations staff. The groundwork was being laid for new ventures that would put Hefner before the public eye. One such was the now defunct TV series, "Playboy After Dark," which Hefner was taping at the time. Another was the opening of the Lake Geneva, Wisconsin resort, which would require Hefner's personal efforts to promote. So the remaking of Hefner began to take shape.

For a while it appeared that he was on the road to a normal life. But there was, and still is, that overwhelming "cause." Here's a guy who should be the happiest man on earth, yet he doesn't seem to be even a normally happy one. Is it normal for a man to (almost) never see daylight? Nowhere within the Mansion, except at the front door, can daylight be seen. (Rosenzweig opens his office window, but Hefner never goes there.) Every window has metal blinds and drapes and is never opened. The conference room—sealed. The halls have no windows. The pool area, the guest rooms, all lack natural light.

Hefner's bedroom is like a sealed capsule. He does a great deal of his work in a round bed, eight and one-half feet in diameter, which revolves or vibrates or who knows what at the mere touch of a button. By rotating the bed toward the bar or the fireplace or the television set, Hefner can simulate going from room to room. On the floor lies a huge polar bear rug. A life-size epoxy sculpture by Frank Gallo of a seated nude girl is passively poised alongside the fireplace. For some reason a TV camera can be trained on the bed. Small refrigerators are scattered throughout his quarters (there is even one in the headboard of his bed) all filled with—you guessed it—Pepsis.

Hefner's main contact with the outside world is still through newspapers, national magazines and television. The eight TV monitors attest to that. Television shows will often be taped for Hefner's later viewing. Hefner was once dubbed "the complete man of electronics" in a magazine article. Anything to avoid face-to-face contact with another human being appears to be his preference.

He carries that out inside his world, too, writing memos rather than talking to people in person. But there is an additional reason—he writes extremely long memos, very few short ones, and he writes them for effect. He knows that it makes an indelible impression on the recipient when he receives a six, eight or ten-page treatise from Hefner. Also, it caresses his ego when he is able to write such a memo on some relatively minor aspect of his empire, one he really couldn't be expected to know anything about.

I remember one of the most interesting memos I received from Hefner was on the subject of Gleneagles, Ltd., a dummy company I set up for Playboy to sell direct mail merchandise through. We planned coupon advertising with pull-out cards in *VIP* magazine and in order not to offend other advertisers, I set up this name-only corporation.

When Hefner learned what I had called it, he wrote me a long, long memo in which he said that to him Gleneagles represented a total contradiction of the *Playboy* concept. He said if you took glen, you came out with something that is a rocky hillside, or a country or rural approach, and that was contrary to the urban nature of *Playboy* and its audience. And the word eagles, he said, represented Americana, superpatriotism and rightwing conservatism. Put them together, he

124

went on, and you have rural super-patriotism of a rightwing, ultra-conservative nature. And that's why he thought the name Gleneagles was bad.

The ad was ready to run and did. I don't like wasting time writing memos so the next time I saw Hefner, I had his memo with me and I had circled the section about the name with a red grease pencil and written across the top of it: "This is bullshit," and I showed it to him. He looked at it and said, "Oh, yes, that thing, well, that's a view," and we dropped it.

Hefner has effectively banished daylight from his impenetrable fortress. Even his DC-9 is blacked out in terms of his own private windows. He seems to want to create his own environment. I'm not saying that he turns into a Count Dracula and shields his face with a cape when he is exposed to daylight. I'm saying that here is a man who has successfully created his own environment and I think he couldn't get by unless he did. Is he insecure? Yes, I think he is. And he has some pretty obsessive needs, some pretty compulsive ones.

What if I can't get along with everybody else's environment? What if I can't live with the rest of the world's habit of being awake in the daytime and sleeping at night? What if I absolutely need to change those things in order to survive? Then something is wrong. Anyone who has rejected everyone else's environment as much as Hefner has must have the need rather than just the desire.

One thing Hefner did during his long period of self-exile was to write the "Playboy Philosophy." It was a mammoth thing, running for 25 installments and probably a quarter-million words.

I think I was one of the very few Playboy executives ever to read the damned thing. I found it interesting mostly because I knew Hefner, but very dated and restrictive in viewpoint. It's tedious, repetitious, and it espouses a set of attitudes that is almost contrary to his own actions.

He writes about openmindedness, a breadth and scope of view regarding a number of matters, but he is as narrow and as restricted in his views as anyone could be.

Anyway, very few people had read it—Anson Mount, Preuss, Spectorsky, of course, but other than that, nobody even knew very much about it, or what it was. All they knew was that Hefner spent a long time writing the thing. Hefner and I discussed it a couple of times, very casually.

Several times we talked about the substance of it and once the fact that he had locked himself away for an extensive period of time to write it and he regretted having done so. He said that he was glad from the standpoint of achieving the result he did. He also thought writing it had changed him. But he regretted the time it had taken, time he could have used doing things he liked or enjoyed.

Time magazine's comment on it in its March 3, 1967, issue was: "Hefner's thesis was that U.S. society had too long and too rigorously suppressed good, healthy heterosexuality. Since its growth had been stunted, Hefner argued, all sorts of perversions flourished in its place. 'You get healthy sex not by ignoring it but by emphasizing it,' he maintains. And the villain at the bottom of all this? Organized religion, announced Hefner, with an unabashed air of discovery. Hefner revived puritanism long enough to condemn it for being as 'stultifying to the mind of man' as Communism or any other totalitarian concept."

A typical working day for Hefner starts with his arising about one or two o'clock in the afternoon. His meetings with other Playboy executives usually start about two hours later. Before that time, however, he will be briefed by Dick Rosenzweig or Bobby Arnstein, his secretary, on pertinent matters in general or the nature of meetings that day.

These meetings begin with such people as Spectorsky, Kessie, Lehrman, Murray Fisher, Sheldon Wax, the editorial people, or he might meet with Preuss, Lownes, Morton, Rosenzweig (and myself, when I was there) on matters pertaining to the club or hotel operations. Or with Preuss and me on circulation promotion and fulfillment, or with Vince Tajiri and John Mastro on the technical quality of the magazine, primarily the graphics.

All of these sessions are always held at the Mansion with

Hefner rarely venturing outside for any. Hefner never went to the Playboy offices because he had the feeling that people should come to him. And where the rest of the Playboy personnel is concerned, I think Hefner feels that he is a public enough figure so that personal confrontation is unnecessary. Does the public really need to see Richard Nixon in the flesh?

The meetings at the Mansion last anywhere from 3 p.m. to 2 a.m., but generally until 10 or 11. They were held in the conference room around a six-foot circular table. The walls are wood-paneled, the floor carpeted. A light-box for studying film negatives is built against one wall. On another wall hangs a cartoon-photograph of model Jean Shrimpton that Hefner finds highly amusing. It's the photographic head of Jean pasted onto a cartoon sketch of a huge-breasted woman's body. The caption states: "What have you done with my body?"

Hefner doesn't take notes at the meetings because Rosenzweig does. In a wild, crazy shorthand he covers the major points. And throughout the meeting Hefner is puffing, tamping, emptying and filling his pipe while he shuffles back and forth to the nearby refrigerator for—a Pepsi. What else? He would always ask if anybody else wanted one. It struck me funny every time we sent Hefner for a Pepsi.

One meeting could go on for many hours, or several short conferences running two hours each could be held during the course of the evening. Dinner was ordered served in the conference room for Hefner and anyone else there at the time. His kitchen staff is on call 24 hours a day.

Meetings are known in advance anywhere from two hours to a month, depending upon the subject matter, who is going to attend, and the importance ascribed to them. Also, whether it's a one-time shot or is regularly scheduled. For example, my sessions with Hefner regarding *VIP* magaine were scheduled once every three weeks. My talks with him on subjects such as the lobby of the building or some public relations effort or some new business venture were sometimes set up at the last minute.

Hefner feels better working at night, as he explains, because the night serves as a "psychological moat" around his domain. It cuts him off from the distractions of the daytime world. In other words, he doesn't have to confront people. There is one point that Hefner overlooks, however, where his executives are concerned. When he begins his full day (night) of work, in mid-afternoon, everyone else in the company has already put in almost a full day. Hefner is rested and rarin' to go just at the time his executives are getting ready to unwind. But this doesn't faze him.

The days I met with Hefner could be extremely long ones for me, beginning at 7 a.m. when I'd get to the office, and ending at midnight or 1 a.m. When his meetings were over, Hefner relaxed, retiring to the Great Hall of the Mansion to play gin rummy with Preuss, or backgammon with someone, or dominoes with Barbi, the girl he was then dating. Or perhaps visiting with a celebrity, Sammy Davis or Hugh O'Brien or Bill Cosby or Shel Silverstein, the cartoonist. So Hefner would entertain from midnight to 4 or 5 a.m., at which time he would retire.

When Hefner changed his life style it wasn't for the sole purpose of longevity. He wanted to see the world and meet the people who couldn't or wouldn't come to see him. But before he could take off to meet the world, he needed two things: his very own mode of transportation and his very own companion. For transportation he got himself a big customized DC-9 jet. For companionship he got himself a real live Barbi doll.

The inaugural flight was long over by the time I went to work at Playboy but I made several trips with Hefner in his jet-black jet, the DC-9 Big Bunny. It is just as luxurious as it has been painted in print.

In fact, it glows. That's the effect of the deep orange carpet and sofas, of course. In contrast are the individual chairs of white styrofoam and black plastic, a tan ceiling and white inner walls.

The first announcement that Playboy Enterprises intended to acquire a jet plane came in 1967 but it didn't become an actuality until much later because of all the extras and custom-built and built-in features. One entire interior was junked because Hefner didn't like it. The Big Bunny can carry 38 and a dozen or so chairs, tables and sofas can be converted into beds for night flights.

Chicago designers Dan Czubak and Gus W. Kostopulos were responsible for the many innovations that make the Big Bunny different from any executive or company plane in existence. Everything is programmed or push-buttoned. It has an inter-plane telephone that Hefner can also use air-to-land.

The forward compartment can be used either for work or for playing games of various types; there's a discotheque area for drinking and dancing. In the rear is Hefner's private compartment with its polarized windows. It also contains an elliptical bed, upholstered in black Himalayan goat leather and covered with a spread of Tasmanian opossum pelts. The custom-contoured sheets are of white silk and retractable armrests form part of the black headboard, which has stereo headsets plugged into it. Casual pillows, orange-covered, are thrown against the headboard. A bathroom is complete with shower.

For the thirsty guest there is a row of liquor dispensers with a bar-in-a-drawer below with ice storage. Video tapes are viewed on seven built-in screens.

The list is endless—this is just a sample.

The only thing that isn't a push-button operation is the service. That's taken care of by specially trained Jet Bunnies. They were culled from the 900 Bunnies who work in the Playboy Clubs and only the most beautiful were called to sky duty. Each of the original seven who accepted the invitation got a $500 wardrobe, attended standard stewardess instruction sessions at Continental Airlines' school in Los Angeles and another special course at Purdue Airlines in Lafayette, Indiana. Purdue operates and services the plane and the girls learned about the exclusive features and how to operate them.

They've also learned gourmet cooking. The plane is equipped with custom ovens and the girls show their skill

129

with prime rib roasts, roast duckling, steaks, crepes and you name it.

The Jet Bunnies wear wet-look black nylon outfits with a mini-dress and matching pants, knee-length stretch boots, a trench coat and a white silk helmet scarf. The Bunny emblem appears on the scarf and on specially designed stewardess wings. Walter Holmes, now of Chicago but born in London, designed the costumes.

The girls are divided into two crews of six each, one in Chicago and one in Los Angeles, with one of each set designated as "senior hostess."

The training was hard, they tell me, but flying around the world made the effort worth it, at least the Bunnies thought so. And that's exactly what Hefner did—began flying around the world. In July 1970 he flew off on that long overdue vacation he had promised himself while he was cooped up all those years. His month-long itinerary included London, Spain, Nairobi, Kenya, Athens, Rome, Venice, Munich, Paris, and Morocco. His entourage included artist Leroy Neiman and, of course, his new-found companion, Barbi Benton.

When *Playboy* did a pictorial spread on Barbi it called her "an outdoor girl by nature." (After being inside so long, one wouldn't expect Hefner to choose an indoor girl.) Hefner prefers to call Barbi "a nice Jewish girl," whom he described to *New York* magazine as being "perfectly innocent, except in her relationship to me (Hefner.)"

Barbi is now 21, but when Hefner met her on the third program of Playboy After Dark she was just 19. She became a regular on the now defunct TV show and was featured as "Barbi Doll," in a nine-page *Playboy* color spread (March 1970 issue), wearing a series of bikini bottoms and various wet or unbuttoned shirts. Barbi has gone on to stardom as the kissing-sweet-breathed girl in Certs' TV commercial—"If he kissed you once, will he kiss you again?" And she also appeared in a movie, *How Did a Nice Girl Like You Get Into This Business?* with a cameo appearance by—that's right— Hugh Hefner.

When Hefner first met Barbi he liked everything about her

except her name. So, he changed it. Barbara Klein became Barbi Benton. The name Klein was not too Jewish, Hefner insisted, but rather too German. Then why didn't he name her Goldberg? That's not too German.

So many people have asked me, "What does Hefner see in this girl, why does he keep her around?" What they mean is why does he put up with her when she's so simple? I'm sure part of the answer is that she must supply Hefner's need for serenity in his environment. But I suppose Hefner really answered the question when he once said, "I like to form things. I'm not attracted to dumb girls, just young girls."

Hefner's basic tastes have always been relatively simple. His favorite drink is Pepsi-Cola, his favorite food is a pork-chop sandwich. So, why shouldn't his favorite girl be Barbi?

Hefner took her to the Las Vegas convention and the day he and I had our long discussion on the Christmas ads, she was walking around the suite in a very, very brief bikini. I noticed her, you bet I did, so maybe her beauty is her saving grace.

Several times, Hefner asked her to make a phone call for him or to contact someone in the hotel and her response each time was that she didn't know his number and Hefner would say look it up. She'd say, well, where? And he'd tell her to try the phone book or call information. This is not a real smart girl who has to be told how to find a telephone number.

Conversation with Barbi is impossible, though I talked "at" her several times, like this:

Me: "Barbi, how do you enjoy Las Vegas?"

Barbi: "It's ho-ot." She's got this little-girl voice and dips and drawls her vowels.

Me: "Do you enjoy gambling?"

Barbi: "Hef doesn't li-ike me to."

Me: "Oh. Have you been to see any of the shows yet?"

Barbi: "Sho-ows?"

Me: "The entertainment, the acts at the various hotels?" (Because I thought she was going to tell me she had just seen "National Velvet.")

Barbi: "Oh, no-o, but we're going toni-ight."

It's hard work, talking with Barbi, but she's a very pleasant, very built, girl. Just a pretty, sweet young thing with some real miniscule brain matter in her lovely head.

One of the most telling instances of her lack of intelligence came at the show that Barbi and Hefner and I and several others attended at the Stardust. It was the Don Adams show and Hefner and Don have been friends for a long time. We were at ringside and I sat on one side of Barbi and Hefner the other. And what absolutely amazed me is that throughout the show, Barbi laughed in all the wrong places and never in the right ones.

Adams would be halfway through a joke, merely establishing the premise, and would not have said anything funny and Barbi would suddenly break out in convulsive laughter. She would quiet down in time for the end of the joke and at the punchline would sit there stonefaced, staring at Adams, while everyone else was hysterically laughing.

All of Playboy's executives speak of her in fairly derisive terms, commenting that she's a goodlooking girl but that she looks like an infant, which she does. She's 21 now and she doesn't carry herself in an adult way. She wears little party dresses like Tricia Nixon Cox, although she's getting a little more high fashion now.

But most people look at her and think, oh, God, is this girl stacked, what a figure or what a beautiful girl or something to that effect. Even if they met her they would be too engrossed in admiring her body to notice the words coming out of her mouth.

Most people never get to the same level of awareness as those at Playboy, of course. I've met the girl so I can relate the specifics of her personality, like the fact that she laughs in the wrong places. I don't think most people are affected by her lack of intelligence and I don't think anybody has ever said in Hefner's hearing that this is a real stupid girl.

Now, he might have seen it if he were openminded. I think then he might say to himself, "Don Adams did kid more about her being nine years old than he might have if I'd brought some older-looking gal."

But he is not openminded and consequently he may not even recognize these nuances I've recorded.

Anyway, Hefner is faithful—in his way—to Barbi. I never knew him to date anyone else except when Barbi was in Europe or California or somewhere not in the immediate vicinity.

One day I was showing him some subscription ads and Barbi was in Europe at the time, I believe filming a movie. Hefner looked longer at one shot than he usually did and said, "Interesting looking girl. Who is she?"

"Just some model," I said carelessly, thinking nothing of Hefner's sudden flash of curiosity.

"She a Playmate?" he asked. I said no.

"Hm, seems to me I've seen her before," he mused.

Still being too inattentive to catch on, I said, "Well, it could be, she's been in other local advertising I understand."

"What did you say her name was?" he asked, and finally the other shoe dropped.

"It's Simone Jabaneau," I said, though I'm not sure now that was the last name. It was a French name.

A couple of days later one of the art directors came in.

"I got a call from Simone," he said, "and guess what? She dated Hefner last night at the Mansion."

"How in hell did that come about?" I asked.

"I guess you told Hefner who she was," he replied, "and he told Tajiri to arrange for her to come over to the Mansion."

She was at the Mansion for the Sunday afternoon movie and things like that. That type of "dating" occurred occasionally but on the whole, I never saw him with any girl except Barbi.

I suppose it is consistent with Hefner's being a "loner" that he seems not to recognize the principles of the conventional family group and also that his attitude toward close business associates is—on the surface, at least—so callous.

His relationship with his parents, for instance, I think is more one of convenience than of reality. Conversationally, he steers away from discussion of any personal or family relationships and the only reason I ever heard the least thing about his children is that we were meeting one evening when his daughter called. He was on the phone with her for about a half-hour and when he hung up he apologized for keeping me waiting and said, "She's a little mixed up and periodically I have to talk to her like a father." The son, David Paul, is 16 or 17 now, the daughter, Christie Ann, a couple of years older.

As far as his executive associates go, he doesn't care anything about them personally—whether they're married, divorced, happy or unhappy, healthy or sick. An extreme example of that is his behavior when Spectorsky was in the hospital with a pretty bad heart attack.

"Well," Hefner said, "I suppose I ought to make one of my rare public appearances and go see Spec in the hospital." This was at the time Spectorsky's illness was at its peak.

"Yeah, Hef," Preuss agreed, "that would be a good idea, I think he would really appreciate it."

"By the way," Hefner said, "how is he?"

"He's coming along," Preuss told him, "we hope he's over the worst of it."

"That's good," Hefner said, with no great interest. He had shown no emotion whatever, no "Christ, it's really a shame he had a heart attack," or "God, I hope he pulls out of it quickly," or "Can we do anything special for him?"

I'm not saying he is a cold-blooded person, but I am saying that in regard to personal and family relationships, he seems that way. Basically, he relates to people only on a business level.

As for friends, Hefner classifies his only business friend as Bernie Cornfeld. It is no accident, as Hefner has explained, that he can count his business friends on one finger. Most of his friends are show business personalities, "creative" people as he prefers to call them. When it comes to mixing with celebrities Hefner gets just as excited as the average man on the street. The highlight of Hefner's vacation trip was the party that was given in his honor at the London Playboy

Club. (He loves the London club and considers it well run.) It was jam-packed with personalities such as Beatle Ringo Starr, actors Peter Sellers and Laurence Harvey, former Grand Prix racer Sterling Moss, film-maker Roman Polanski, artists and models—Hefner was in his glory.

As I got to know Hefner better, I realized there were two Hugh Hefners—the public one and the real one. The public Hefner wants to appear as a man who takes what he is doing seriously, but who doesn't take himself seriously. Well, Hefner is serious about everything, especially himself. He takes himself seriously from his very precise attention to dress when he's going out in public to his adverse reactions to anything but the most positive publicity.

Hefner tries to protect his public image to the utmost possible. When, for example, he agreed to an interview with his old employer, *Esquire* magazine, in December 1970, he did so only after he secured the right to "complete approval" of the finished interview, including the editorial precede. *Esquire* agreed. The interview was favorable and pretty straight and lacked the irreverent touch that is *Esquire's* forte.

Sometime in the spring of 1970 Hefner was scheduled to appear on the Dick Cavett TV show along with two representatives of the Women's Liberation movement and Dr. Mary Calderone, the head of the Sex Information and Education Council of the U.S. The Cavett producers decided not to use Calderone on the show. When Hefner found out, he panicked. He refused to appear without her. She was a valuable addition, Hefner said, because she understood his views regarding women's liberation and sexuality.

In private, however, he told me that Calderone would provide a foil for him and that he was insecure about going on without her. In other words, with Calderone, the odds against the two liberation women were somewhat better—at least in Hefner's mind. Finally, Cavett agreed to allow Calderone on the show and Hefner appeared. Hefner felt it was his best TV appearance. If it wasn't, at least it was his most secure. He had Calderone and, of course, his beloved pipe.

135

Incidentally, when Cavett introduced Hefner he said, "We're going to snatch his pipe away and watch him roll up into a little ball." Thank God Cavett didn't do it.

Where Hefner's prejudices were concerned, he never indicated any for reasons of color or religion. But when it came to sex, that was a different matter. I suppose you would classify him as a true male chauvinist. He feels women are merely objects and of a lesser level of intelligence than men. For instance, he was impressed by a story written about him by Julie Baumgold in *New York* magazine. But he couldn't just talk about the merits of the story and leave it at that. He said, "Huh, shocking she could write such a good story, after all, just a woman." He said many disparaging things like that.

In fact, the one major article in *Playboy* on the Women's Liberation movement was written by Morton Hunt, and that only after a solicited article written by a woman on the same subject was turned down by Hefner. The fair approach would have been to give both the male and female viewpoints. But Hefner wouldn't allow it.

To the public, Hefner always tries to project himself as an open person. This is not so. He doesn't wear his emotions on his sleeve. He can be open and blunt with his underlings when he's telling them what he thinks in terms of how something should be done and how instead it has been done stupidly. He can do this because it doesn't cost him anything emotionally. But he could never bring himself to constructively help an individual who was doing a poor job if to do so required face-to-face contact. He would rather have the person fired by remote control. He gets rid of people who bug him.

But the "off with their heads" attitude never did apply to the top people at Playboy. That, as I have already stated, is because they were so loyal to Hefner. And he sets great store by loyalty.

As for Hefner's sense of humor, well, you don't exactly break up when you meet him. His humor is more on the macabre or sadistic side. He thought, for example, what was happening to his personal friend, Bernie Cornfeld, former head of Investors Overseas Services whose $2 billion financial

136

empire crumbled beneath him, was hilarious. (Cornfeld at one time had been called the "Hugh Hefner of Europe." I don't know what he's called now.) Only once did I see Hefner really howl and that was at a photograph taken of a Bunny on water skis at Miami Beach. The girl's bunnytail became water-logged and was pulling her bikini off, exposing her behind. Hefner chuckled over that for a long time.

Chapter 12
Don't Give Me That Same Old Line

Before I took over as director of mail marketing, they had the idea that the Playboy Preferred list meant that every merchandise offer had to be related to sex or to a male-female relationship. So the offer might be a bar, a bearskin rug, things like that. Every offer was centered around the implication that you lay the girl you're with and use this merchandise to help you do so.

Playboy by-products are consumer products bearing the rabbit trademark that Playboy so jealously guards. (The company spends thousands of dollars each year to broaden the protection of its trademark, registered in more than 40 countries.) The products, manufactured by outside suppliers licensed by Playboy, are sold through the clubs and hotels and by mail order. The first by-product was the *Playboy Annual*, introduced in November 1954. It was a collection of cartoons, articles and fiction from the first twelve issues of *Playboy*.

When I took over there were 80 items in the line that

included jewelry (bracelets, anklets, pins, earrings), men's clothing (sweaters, ski and golf jackets, sweat shirts), leather goods (cigarette cases, billfolds) and a wide assortment of accessories (golf putters, pipes, lighters, Playmate jigsaw puzzles, carving boards, beach towels, address books, perfume, study pillows). It added up to more than $3 million a year in revenues.

The best-selling product over the years has been a Baby Doll, candy-striped nightgown and cap in red and white flannel. It sells for $6. (Teenagers buy it through the ads in the magazine. A study of who buys merchandise through the magazine revealed that the average buyer was 17.5 years old.) The second hottest selling item is the Playboy garter, followed by the stuffed rabbit.

No attention was paid to the fact that Playboy keyholders eat and drink and sleep and do everything else that non-keyholders do and so here they were, saturated with narrow, restrictive concepts, forgetting that these people buy cookware and dishes and binoculars and fur parkas and all sorts of products that have always been very successful.

I wanted to change that.

I had ideas about the direct response offerings of the rabbit-identified merchandise. These ideas resulted in a long session with Hefner at which Preuss and Rosenzweig were present.

We were reviewing a number of new things that I had done without Hefner's prior concurrence, such as killing about 25 percent of the product line that Hefner had either personally created or helped to create many years earlier. Hefner wanted to know why I had made these changes. In some cases new designs of comparable products were adopted. In other cases, the products were killed outright.

For one thing, I killed about 14 items in the gold jewelry line. These items—anklets, charm bracelets, conventional bracelets, a necklace, earrings, a pin, several other things—all featured a large rabbit's head electroplated in a yellow color to simulate gold. I thought they were all ugly and dated.

And as for the clothing items, I wanted to reduce the

rabbit badge on the outside to a label on the inside. I felt the rabbit insignia on, say, a sweater or a jacket, distracted from the overall look of the item.

Anyway, sales were only moderately successful. They had sold well years before but tastes change, in this case for the better. These things might have been great when girls wore four crinolines under long skirts—seriously, the line had the look of the early '50s about it. You would expect to see the Playboy cufflinks on a pink shirt with charcoal gray saddle-stitching around the collar, hot stuff in the '50s.

Nothing had been changed for fifteen years and when I saw the line, I asked a couple of people why it was there. And the best answer I could get was:

"Hefner won't allow any Playboy products to be discontinued—he wants everything that was ever created to remain in every gift shop and every club and hotel and, further, he wants them advertised as often as possible by using filler ads in the magazine."

"That's not a good enough reason," I said. "Has anyone realized that they represent the identity that the corporation is attempting to establish? Has anybody determined whether or not they contribute to the public awareness of Playboy as a progressive, contemporary, positive business organization? Or whether they make it look like a place that is selling every kind of trash that you can find in any flea market."

"That's incidental," they said, "because Hefner wants it."

I issued an order to kill those items, not to run any more ads on them, and to attempt to get rid of the inventory through some other channel. Then I found designers to redesign the products that were in worthwhile categories. When the new designs arrived, I asked Alan Rosenblatt, director of purchasing, to order an initial quantity of each of the fifteen or twenty new designs, a few thousand of each.

So all this got back to Hefner through Rosenblatt, one of Hefner's schoolmates. He was sure that Hefner would never allow it and I said, "Look, if you won't place the order I'll have somebody else in the company do it."

Rosenblatt must have thought along the lines of "I'll get

back at him, I'll let Hefner know all of this is going on" and he sent Hefner samples of the new items, saying in a memo, "I just thought you ought to be informed that all of these new products have been brought into the line. Byer did it."

That was when Hefner's secretary called and said he was terribly upset and wanted to see me. I went to the Mansion and Hefner said, "What you've done may be better than what we had, although personally I don't think so, but I want to know why you did it."

"The reason I did it," I told him, "is because you made me responsible for handling this line of merchandise and trying to build it into something positive. Also, sales have been going down the last two years because the public has caught on to the fact that this stuff looks like junk."

"I don't believe that," Hefner said.

I brought out the sales figures for the last three years, very extensive figures tallied on every single item by club, hotel, and ad, not only in terms of sales revenue but profits, number of units, dollars of revenue and so on. And the records showed that for the two previous years, sales had been drastically reduced. Hefner said he was really surprised.

But, surprised or not, we got into a hassle over whether I should have redesigned the line and what happened then made me realize how really, totally loused up business is in so many companies.

Hefner buzzed the intercom for Bobbie Arnstein, his secretary, and asked if anyone else was around. She said Joe (the houseman) and Mary (one of the other secretaries), so he sent her to get them.

"Now," said Hefner, "we have here two piles of jewelry, here's one and here's the other, which I personally prefer, but that's neither here nor there. Tell me which you prefer."

The second secretary asked, "Mr. Hefner, which did you say you prefer?" And I told her, "He prefers this one over here," because he had said it in a casual manner and none of them had caught it. Rosenzweig and I chuckled because he had told them he preferred the new design.

Only the houseman didn't follow Hefner's lead.

"Mr. Hefner," he said, "I don't care what you say but personally I prefer this" and he pointed to the old-style stuff.

Both of the secretaries said there was no question, these are far superior, really great, and they pointed to the new items.

That was two to one and Hefner, apparently hoping he could at least even it up, said, "Go get one of the cooks in here," and this dumpy old lady came shlepping in.

"Which of these do you prefer," Hefner said, "you can have either, which do you want?" And she looked and said, "Ah-h, I like this one," and she pointed to the new stuff.

That made it three to one and Hefner said, "Well, I don't know how you clued these people in on which way to answer, but— "

So, at that point, my future was greatly enhanced because I had been exonerated by two secretaries and one cook. Preuss and Rosenzweig, of course, hadn't said boo. Dick was probably fearful of being caught between disagreeing with Hefner and my wrath being such that I wouldn't tell him where I got my newest shirts.

Hefner, acceding to the informal court's opinion, went along with the rest of the products I had summarily put into the line.

Working up an ad campaign, as I did for this line of products, is an enthralling part of my business. Picking an objective, starting from nothing, creating something that will persuade people to do what I want them to, or make them want to do it, following it through to completion and then sitting back and awaiting results, awaiting the public's decision on my baby—it's a heady feeling.

Take the 1970 Christmas subscription ad campaign for which I was responsible, the largest single subscription solicitation push of the year. It started in March, when the result of the 1969 advertising in the October, November, December and January 1970 issues was analyzed from computer reports prepared by the fulfillment staff.

All of the orders received from each of the ads and from each of the test splits within the ads (test split means that code numbers are inserted that indicate the different markets the same ad is sent to) were analyzed in a meeting with Preuss, a couple of the fulfillment people, the promotion director, his art director, the copy chief and several others. But prior to this main session, held in Preuss' office, I met with all of the promotion staff involved in it in my own office.

What we were looking for was the broad pattern of response, by season or by issue; what combination of ingredients within the publication did best—that is, two subscription envelopes and four insert cards and one two-page spread and one coupon in the back of the book, or whatever.

We tried to recognize or decide what had achieved what results and why, and then it was up to me to incorporate the "why" into the 1970 advertising.

Next came involvement in the creation of a series of new advertisements that struck me as likely to improve sales.

The reason that campaign succeeded is due to one thing and that was a full realization on my part of what attracts people to *Playboy* magazine. It is the magazine's overpowering, sensual sexuality. Perhaps we are all voluptuaries at heart, but I felt that was the key to the subscription advertising in the magazine.

That idea came to me from reading the correspondence reports prepared by the editorial department, saying that 4,273 people have written in on this subject and 4,012 on that subject and two on something else and so on. It is done on a continuing basis and used for planning editorial matter and yet the promotion and advertising people had overlooked the big ingredient revealed in the reports that could double or triple the results. I don't think any marketing director had ever read them.

Anyway, the most read "article" in *Playboy* is the centerfold; second is the back of the book sex article and the third the front of the book sex article. After that came the Playboy interview, the service article and then the other regulars, like the forum, the jokes page, the fiction.

When I came to the conclusion that *Playboy* was bought

mainly for the nude pictures, I decided that since we had available for the subscription ad a two-page, full-color space, I would make it the most sexually attractive nude I possibly could, one that would be every bit as good as an editorial nude. I felt this had to attract attention, had to make the reader aware of why he was buying *Playboy* and an accompanying form would make it easy and convenient for him to subscribe.

So I took the girl out of the classic ad-type pose with mistletoe or wreath and posed her on a huge Christmas package, as if she were the seal. She was spread across the two pages, whereas in previous years the girl was only partially nude on one page and there was a great clutter of copy on both pages. All I put with my nudes was an imperative command to the consumer to subscribe to the magazine as a Christmas gift. We threw in the coupon and the returns looked like this:

	1969-70	1970-71	% Increase
October	37,054	72,191	95
November	29,589	58,148	97
December	41,850	78,912	89
January	24,333	64,098	163

When I said before that I was involved in the creation of this series of ads, I meant that I laid out the basic principles of each of the four ads—actually it was six, to provide a choice of four—and the basic graphic and copy approach that I wanted taken. My directions to the promotion staffers were specific to the point of telling them that for one ad I wanted a headline that had a double meaning, referring to buying a gift and getting a girl, and I wanted it to tie in with a photograph of one of the Playmates as the ornament on top of a Christmas package. But the promotion staffers did better for me than that—they turned out four headlines that I thought put over that idea tastefully. They were:

October, "Give the Gift to Curl Up With."

November, "The Shape of Things to Come for Christmas . . . "

144

December, "Capture a Christmas Original!"

January, "Still Time to Tie Up Good Wishes With Playboy."

Some of the promotion people kept saying, "Well, this isn't the way we've done it in the past," but the art director, Don Swanson, welcomed the chance to try something new.

Anyway, Swanson or somebody from promotion—I was working without a promotion director because Mort Pollock had left and Futch wasn't back in that area yet—would come back with a rough comprehensive (drawing) and copy from the copy writer. We would decide what, if anything, was wrong with them or could be changed for the better and they would then be returned for final copy and comprehensives. It would be set in type and test photographs taken of the model in the approximate situation that we were going to use.

I chose the models from among the previous year's Playmates. For example, for the October issue I picked Sharon Clark, who was to become 1971 Playmate of the Year; for November, Claudia Jennings (1970 Playmate of the Year); Chris Koren, who had small breasts, for December, and Carol Imhof, who had giant breasts, for January 1971. We had to film Carol—who is now a Bunny at the Chicago club—on her back and Chris on her stomach, which was the only way her breasts showed at all. Problems, always problems.

So final copy and comprehensives were done on this in the form of a finished kinetic print and I reviewed it with Preuss.

Up to that point, I had spent, for each of the six ads, approximately $3,000 in photography and $3,000 in prints and type, layout time and other necessities, a total of $36,000 for the 1970 ads.

Preuss looked at them and said, "I don't think Hefner will go for any of them, so you'd better be prepared to go back to the old format."

These were the ads that Hefner and I spent an afternoon discussing during the salesmen's convention in Las Vegas, when I was so elated to have challenged and won out over a long-standing tradition at Playboy.

I'll never forget that meeting. It started off with Hefner's initial reaction that "this isn't what we do." He then pondered the ads spread out before us, lit his pipe and said:

"Steve, these are drastically different from anything we have ever done in the past. They are also better. But perhaps we should stay with our past efforts because we know for certain they work."

"They are different," I agreed, adding, "they use the framework of the past ads but they are more contemporary. The photography has been taken especially for these ads." We began to review the transparencies.

And then I went into the copy, how the approaches had been changed, assuming an older, more sophisticated, more educated audience. I began reading the copy of the November ad aloud: "The Shape Of Things To Come for Christmas ... Enticing beauties like Playmate of the Year Claudia Jennings ... spicy fiction and hard-hitting commentary ... colorful tours through the worlds of music, food, travel and fashion ... provocative interviews and rib-tickling humor ... " I argued with Hefner, pointing out the logic of going with what we both felt was a better approach, and taking our chances. After nearly six hours of hassling, Hefner finally agreed.

"All right, Steve, let's go with the new ads, but only on one condition."

"What's that?" I asked.

"I want to test one of the old ads against one of the new approaches. And we should use the ads that have the greatest similarity to one another."

We decided to test the third of the four-ad series. Hefner and I bet $100 on which ad would do better, the old or the new. (The results were never known because the respective subscription return envelopes were coded improperly. But I can assure you, except for that, one of us would have collected even though I had left.)

In terms of cost, the new ad approach was no small-change thing. The cost for just the printed matter, art, envelopes and reply cards was at least $400,000.

I was elated because of my success in changing one of the

longest-standing traditions at Playboy. And I also was some-what dismayed because some of my thoughts about Hefner were confirmed at that meeting. At the onset, he showed his obstinate desire to cling to past norms, either because he felt more secure with them or because he had created them. But Hefner was alone. There was no one around to agree with him, to reinforce his ego. There was just me and my decision had already been made. It was then I realized the most effective way to approach Hefner was one-to-one.

No specific budget had been allotted for the Christmas ad campaign, so the $36,000 came out of the department budget, which was done as most corporate budgets are done—you look at what was spent the year before and add 10 percent across the board and that's your new budget. That's how budgets are arrived at—you go through all these figures, all these calculations and all the time you know you're just trying to come up to what you want, which is what you spent last year plus 10 percent in case you crap around more than last year.

You begin learning the results a week after the issue appears, in a format showing the specific effort, the code number of the ad or the card, quantity of magazines in which it was placed, the response to each offer, the percentage that response represents, the cost of the promotion and the cost per subscription sold.

Actually, my battle to change advertising approaches start-ed while I was still director of mail marketing. I wondered why nudes were featured only in the Christmas ads. After all, statistics proved they had far better results than the others throughout the year. True, they were keyed to gift subscrip-tions and it was Christmas time. But I couldn't help thinking that the use of nudes was a factor. There was only one way to find out—run an ad featuring a nude in other than a Christmas issue. It was as simple as that, or so I thought.

But what could be the reason, I mused, that nudes had been used only during that period of the year. I couldn't think of a sound one, so I asked. And the answer, though typical, was hard to believe. It was something to the effect

147

that Hefner only likes nudity at Christmas.

I took the matter up with Mort Pollock, who was then HMH promotion manager.

"I'm sorry, Steve, but I can't go along with you on using nudes unless you get a note from Hefner approving it," said Pollock, puffing on a pipe. I had absentmindedly picked up one of his pipes and upon hearing his comment I thundered, "Oh, for Christ's sake," slamming my hand—and the pipe—down on his desk. The pipe shattered.

"You broke my pipe, you broke my pipe," he keened, so mournfully I'd have laughed if I hadn't been so annoyed.

Perhaps my exasperation shook him or perhaps it was to prevent me from breaking any more pipes, but after my outburst Pollock hastily agreed to cooperate without a note from Hefner. He accepted my apology and I assured him that from then on his pipes would be safe.

The ad design I accepted I called the "fetal" ad. It was a full-color photograph of a nude girl sitting jackknifed, the upper part of her legs almost touching her breasts, her arms clasping her knees and her face resting on her arms. It was scheduled to run in the April 1970 issue, but was completed the previous November. We worked about five months in advance. Just before the issue was to be printed, Preuss saw a proof and called me to his office.

"Has this had Hefner's ok?" asked Preuss, flashing the proof before me.

"No," I said, in the most innocent-sounding tone I could muster.

"Why not?"

"I didn't know I had to get Hefner's approval," I lied, maintaining my air of innocence but hoping Preuss hadn't spoken with anyone in the promotion department.

"But you know that any new ads have to get his ok," Preuss accused me, his eyes darting from the proof to my face and back to the proof. He wasn't really angry, just frustrated.

"Well, Bob, I'm sure he'll see the proofs and if he doesn't like them, that will be that. I can talk to him about it then."

"I'm not even sure we should antagonize him by showing him the ad in proof form," dithered Preuss.

"Antagonize him?"

"The ad is so totally different. We only use nudity and color in the Christmas ads," putting out his cigarette and snapping his fingers nervously.

"Wait a minute, who told you that, Bob?" I asked, straightening up in my chair.

"Hefner has ruled on that in the past," answered Preuss.

"When?"

"Oh, it must have been a couple, three years ago."

"I don't believe he ever meant it to be a permanent policy," I said. "I don't think he ever said to you, 'Bob, I only want to use nudity and color at Christmas because it is really right then. Other than at Christmas it offends me.' "

"No, don't be stupid, of course it wasn't anything like that. He said we should reserve it for the holidays because it was most effective then." Preuss was now a bit irritated. He lit another cigarette, drew deeply and exhaled a cloud of smoke that hung just above our heads.

"What are you talking about?" I asked. "You mean to say we'll do something below par eight months out of the year because there are always those four months in which we excell?"

"No, no, you just don't understand," said Preuss, exhaling another cloud.

"You're right, I don't understand."

"Well, let me . . . " A knock at Preuss' door interrupted him before he could finish the sentence. It was his secretary.

"I thought as long as Steve was here, you might want to see this," she said, handing Preuss a memo from Hefner. It read, "I don't know who is responsible for the April subscription ad, but whoever it is should certainly be commended. It is one of the best such ads I've ever seen us produce. Please give whoever is responsible my congratulations." He carboned Spectorsky on it.

"Well," said Preuss, clearing his throat, "that answers that. If Hefner had seen that ad prior to proof form he might have had some second thoughts about it. So I'm glad we took that approach." Preuss' reference to "we" rang in my ears like a Chinese gong. I excused myself and left.

Hefner's response to the ad apparently hit the grapevine because in the weeks that followed I received much better cooperation from my cohorts in the promotion department.

But the soft-pedal switch I tried next brought me bang up against Hefner and once again I had to rely on results to prove to him that I knew what I was doing.

The April ad pulled in more than 28,000 subscriptions and for May I ran one I had created some months earlier that I called the Gloria ad and it was a hard-sex approach, too. I called it the Gloria ad because I didn't know the model's name. But she struck me as being very buxom with dark brown hair and deep dark eyes—almost Italian looking—and I thought her name should be Gloria. The four-color ad pictured Gloria in a close-up sort of leaning forward. The pose accentuated her already noticably large breasts that were pointing toward the subscription coupon. The ad headline merely said "choice!" and was followed by copy that stated: "Make it yours—make it *PLAYBOY*. It's the 'in' thing to do . . . and more than 5,000,000 men who have made *PLAYBOY* their number one choice in man-sized entertainment agree . . . " The rest of the copy went on to highlight the various features of the magazine, the *Playmate* foldouts, the fiction, cartoons, fashion, food, automotive features, interviews, and film reviews. The people who read *Playboy* for the pictures are more attracted to this kind of ad than any other. And I don't blame them.

The Gloria ad resulted in between 32,000 and 33,000 subscriptions whereas the ad of the previous May had only culled 12,000. For June I used a Buck Brown cartoon featuring Grandma and we totaled 26,000 to 27,000 from that.

But it occurred to me, in the midst of all this success with the nudist approach, that perhaps there should be a break and a type of ad that would appeal to other elements of our readership, to those who didn't subscribe for the nude pictorials but for other features—fiction, travel, reviews, etc.

That was the rationale behind the "Perfection" ad. It's a subtle, soft, delicate portrayal of a boy and a girl in a boat floating in a lagoon. It's all in muted colors and the only print on the page says "Perfection in people, thoughts, beauty and smiles. Just for you . . . from *PLAYBOY*. Subscribe today." That's all. There's no coupon imprint but there is a subscription card bound in the magazine toward the back.

Hefner was away on a trip while this ad was being created and by the time he returned and saw it, it was too late to kill it, as he wanted to do. He was upset and he disagreed forcefully with me on the rationale, the approach, on everything about the ad.

"You don't have to give people a rationale to subscribe," he argued. "People know that *Playboy* uses nudity only within the broader limits of its total concept."

During a thoughtful pause his eye fell on the "Perfection" presentation. "It's too covert, it doesn't get the point across," he went on. "What do you do about it? There isn't even a coupon."

I kept quiet. I wanted him to talk himself out and I didn't feel it was necessary to do as I ordinarily did in a disagreement with Hefner. That is, to present the merits of my case in a dozen different ways to try to convince him that something I proposed would accomplish what I said it would.

Once was enough this time, I thought, because the ad had run, there was damn-all he could do to stop it now. *Playboy* had never gone to this romantic, sentimental soft-sell but what of it? That didn't mean it wouldn't work and I was confident it would. I didn't need to hard-sell the soft-sell.

So the "Perfection" ad ran as a national A-B split. That means every other copy of the issue had the "Perfection" ad pitted against the Gloria ad as a test, to see which would appeal to more people and bring in more subscribers.

But while Hefner was lamenting that he "knew we shouldn't have gone to this approach" and saying "I really think it's bad," I was thinking I had to make sure that if the ad did well he knew about it.

151

I kept a close watch on returns and while the response opened up gradually, pretty soon it was crystal clear that "Perfection" was out-pulling Gloria—not by a huge margin, but by more than enough to be the winner.

When the pattern was clear, I took the figures to a meeting at the Mansion and read them to Hefner, while he sat puffing away.

"I don't believe in figures," he said when I had finished. "Anyway, there's a mistake there somewhere. It must have been coded wrong."

"Come on, it wasn't coded wrong. How come every other time you believe in figures and this time you don't?"

"Well, at least check it out," he said shortly.

I checked them out until they squeaked. I got a duplicate of the microfilms of a mass of the actual orders and took the stack to Hefner and threw it on the table.

"And here's a more current report," I told him. "Here's a report week by week showing percentages of each ad."

Hefner reluctantly examined the evidence and then said, "I guess we can all be wrong now and then."

If it was an apology it was a weak and graceless one, but admitting he is wrong was never Hefner's long suit.

Another problem that had always intrigued me was that of the attitude of the major airlines toward advertising in *Playboy*. Their excuse for refusing to include us in their budget was that they didn't like *Playboy's* image. Finally it popped into my mind that there might be a back door we could go through that would provide our salesmen with a telling reply to that argument.

I managed to wangle the sale of 28,000 one-year subscriptions at the bulk price, $5, to TWA. They were to be placed on both domestic and international flights. I took this $140,000 plum to Howard Lederer, advertising director.

"Howard," I said jubilantly, "this will give your salesmen an unanswerable riposte to TWA's 'we don't like your image' attitude."

"I don't see how," he said sourly.

"Just think about it a minute. Now your salesmen can say

that TWA thinks enough of the magazine to buy 28,000 subscriptions for distribution on its planes. So it cannot possibly object to the magazine's image any longer."

"I don't think we ought to sell them the subscriptions," Lederer said.

"But why not?" I had visions of $140,000 flying out the window instead of on TWA planes.

Lederer's answer had to come off the top of his head, it was so weak.

"Well, I look upon it more as a negative than a positive. If TWA passengers find *Playboy* magazine on the planes, then they'll stop buying copies at the airport newsstands. I'm afraid that will incense the newsdealers and they will stop selling the magazine."

"Howard," I said carefully, "have the newsdealers at the airports stopped carrying *Life* and *Time* and *Newsweek*?"

"No, but *Playboy* is such a big source of revenue to them that they'll probably feel differently toward it than toward any of the other magazines."

When I finally gave up trying to convert him to my view, the only concession he had made was that he would take it up with his staff and let me know how they felt about it.

I waited for what I thought was a reasonable time and then went ahead with the order. Subscriptions were my field, not Lederer's; I had only wanted to do him a favor.

Several months later I was talking to one of the ad salesmen and because I genuinely wanted to know I asked him how he could have agreed with Howard about the TWA subscriptions.

"What TWA subs?" he inquired, alert at once because he'd been trying for so long to break down the airlines' resistance.

"You know," I told him, "the 28,000 subscriptions that TWA purchased and that are going on their flights now."

"When did this happen? I don't know anything about this," and he was getting angry.

"You and Howard haven't discussed it?"

"This is the first I've heard of it, dammit." He was boiling and rightfully so. It was money out of his pocket.

So, I thought, as he stormed off to find Lederer, Howard never even took it up with the ad salesmen responsible for travel advertising.

Eventually, I heard what happened when the salesman got to Lederer. Howard asked him not to bring the matter up with TWA. "It would just stir up flames," he said. "You sit back and wait and don't worry. Some day you'll get plenty of TWA advertising." The salesman was fit to be tied, particularly because he was smart enough to know that if he could break one of the airlines, the others would follow.

Reflecting on this episode now, I think one reason Lederer made decisions of this kind is that he could allude to one of Hefner's dearest beliefs—the don't rock the boat theme. When any of his actions were questioned, Lederer often said, "Well, Hef, I'm afraid that if we do this or try that, it may seriously disturb our present fine advertisers." And that's been effective because Hefner definitely is sold on the policy of "why do anything different than what has brought us success in the past?"

One advertising proposal that interested me was suggested by Playboy's then newly hired ad agency, Rink Wells & Associates of Chicago. At the Las Vegas sales convention Rink Wells presented a media campaign geared to enhancing Playboy's corporate identity by sponsoring—on television—a major sporting event such as a professional football game or basketball game or a golf tournament. This type of approach would promulgate Playboy's total identity in terms of the magazine, clubs, and hotels. But the idea was shot down because, as Lederer explained, for Playboy to advertise on TV was demeaning to print media in general and consequently, contradictory to *Playboy's* own sales efforts. But *Newsweek* and *Time* frequently advertise on radio and in newspapers, and the *Wall Street Journal* has been using TV for some time. Their advertising efforts in competitive media do not appear to have hurt them. It was no use arguing the point with Lederer because he had the full support of his ad salesmen and they weren't about to back anyone else.

Another advertising approach I wanted to develop was that

of trading out subscription advertising space with *Cosmopolitan*, the popular woman's magazine. In a trade-out between two magazines, each gives the other a free page of advertising. It's a mutual exchange of advertising space that offers each respective magazine a crack at a new market for no cash outlay.

The idea came to me while I was reviewing the research files on Christmas advertisements of past years. I found that 38 percent of the responses to the ad offerings came from women. I foresaw a worthwhile increase if the presentation appeared in *Cosmopolitan*, which appeals to women on much the same basis as *Playboy* appeals to men. I put this idea aside as something to develop later because it was a radical departure for *Playboy* that would require a major battle to get through. And I just didn't have the time to take on another one.

Chapter 13
Big Business Decisions

"Retailing isn't the end of business I like to be in; we earn more by making things than just selling them. Young's proposal is a superior one and appears to have a great potential for profit but what Preuss told you is right. I think a one-on-one business is old-fashioned and contradicts the Playboy image."

With those words Hefner chopped off a good business proposition and gave a prime example of how a major corporation is at the mercy of the logic patterns, the prejudices, the personality and character of the corporate head if he wields the power that Hefner does.

So I had to go back to Shelby Young, then vice president-regional manager of the Allied Radio Shack Division of Tandy Corp., and tell him Playboy Enterprises was not interested in his beautifully thought-out plan.

What Hefner calls a one-on-one business, incidentally, is a retail business in which the consumer is waited upon by a sales person.

Young, who has a superb reputation in the consumer

sound electronics distribution field, came to me with an idea for getting Playboy into that business by starting a chain of retail outlets to be called the Playboy Audio Centers.

He brought me a complete architect's prototype of the store layouts; ad formats for an advertising campaign which were quite well done; and a complete financial prospectus on sales, expenses and profits for the first five years. It was an extremely well-planned program, very accurate, from what I could tell, and very positive.

I took it first to Preuss and he stalled. Finally, when I forced him to, he told me it was not in the framework of what Hefner wanted so there was no point in pursuing it. That's when I went to Hefner and struck out.

Hefner struck me out a second time on another retailing idea I presented. I had put together, with the Pleetway Sleepwear Corp., a line of contemporary men's sleepwear made up of pajamas, robes, lounging outfits and jumpsuits. I wanted to market the line through retail stores rather than through the clubs and hotels. The response to the line was highly favorable from the finer department stores in the Chicago area. So I sent samples to the Mansion and told Rosenzweig I wanted to discuss them with Hefner.

Rosenzweig called and said, "Hef doesn't want to have anything to do with pajamas that look like that."

"What the hell does he know about pajamas?" I yelled. "He only knows the kind he wears and they're horrible, they're thirty years old."

But Rosenzweig stood his ground, reiterating that Hefner was dead set against it. "Oh, for Christ's sake, all right," I finally moaned. But I told Rosenzweig we were probably passing up about a million and a half or two million dollars in sales. That didn't faze him and the matter was ended.

There was no use beating a dead horse with Hefner because he either liked something and went with it, or he didn't. It was never a problem to make him understand. In fact, of all the Playboy people I dealt with, Hefner caught on to situations more quickly than any. I realized his ability to get straight to the core of things about a week after I joined

157

Playboy. I was asked to attend a new venture meeting.

A demonstration of an audio-visual cassette system was being conducted at the Mansion by Motorola, Inc. It was October 1969 and everybody in the electronics industry was babbling wildly about the bright future of the audio-visual cassette. It would make home movie equipment and conventional cassette recorders obsolete. Some believed that eventually it would even replace television. Playboy's role would be that of financier and developer of the programming for the system. Most of the Playboy executives attending the demonstration were urging Playboy's involvement in this new communications area. Everyone was gung-ho except Hefner.

"I think this system is still several years away, from the standpoint of development and marketing," said Hefner after hearing everyone else's views on the subject.

It was one of the few times I didn't air my opinion. I was ignorant on the subject. And as it turned out, he was far more perceptive than those around him. There were more than a dozen manufacturers with nine different systems, of which six did not work with any of the others. In other words, there was no conformity of audio-visual hardware in the industry. This fact was borne out months after Hefner had realized it.

But on balance I would say it was Hefner's ego that clouded his judgment in many business ventures. At times he just simply ignored perceptivity and intuition, all for the sake of seeking status in the business world.

It wasn't, however, only Hefner's ego that got in the way of new ventures. It was the egos of other Playboy executives as well. How many years ago did Playboy announce its plans to go back into the executive tour business or travel business? It never happened. Talked about going into the executive jet and yacht charter business? That never happened, either. Going into other magazines? Into other avenues of its editorial features such as the rock or jazz concert tour business? Talked about getting into the photography business? (Who could better tell the public how to photograph nudes?)

Efforts have been made to get some of these projects

moving but somewhere between proposal and implementation they faded away. Why? Because of ego. There is a reluctance by some executives to let go of certain responsibilities in their areas. But, after all, they are only aping the top man himself, who is the stingiest of all in letting go the reins.

One executive, for example, went so far as to represent himself as Playboy's marketing director several months after I had been in the post. He was negotiating with a foreign firm for the development of a Playboy Club on wheels. The proposed double-decker cruiser was to be used as a shuttle between Chicago's O'Hare airport and the Playboy resort at Lake Geneva, Wisconsin. Club members would ride the sixty miles to Geneva in a holiday atmosphere that would include facilities for drinking, relaxing and card-playing—the whole luxurious works.

Initially, the idea seemed feasible. From a cost standpoint, however, it was totally impractical. The cruiser was to cost a half-million dollars to build and had a life expectancy of only three years. To break even it would have to be fully occupied and shuttling twenty hours a day. That was an impossibility.

By the time Preuss and I found out about the clandestine negotiations, the executive had already vetoed the project.

Renowned British model Jean Shrimpton was to be the voice of Playboy for a course on the beauty secrets of the Playmates. The beauty course consisted of cassettes, books and a line of health and beauty aid products. The products, used by international beauties, would come from all over the world. Jean was all set to participate, but the venture died. Spectorsky killed it because it was a special editorial project over which he would have no control.

Vince Tajiri wouldn't permit the presentation of photography courses from Playboy's photographers. He said it would "allow other magazines to pick up Playboy's valuable techniques." The reason for Tajiri's apathy, I later learned, centered upon his role. He was only to be one of several photographers involved. Spectorsky was going to head it up, whereas Tajiri wanted to be tabbed as editor. Consequently,

159

Tajiri's lack of enthusiasm brought things to a halt.

Playboy was also considering going into the frozen convenience food business, but that plan quickly thawed, too. The food line made a great deal of sense because of Playboy's rather affluent market. The line could be sold in retail stores as well as in the Playboy Clubs. Or a club member could sign up for various foods and they would be shipped directly to his residence.

Frozen steaks via direct mail is a booming business and one that has a lot of room for competition. But Playboy's line was to include more than just frozen meats. Well, the plan got as far as Bill Lassiter, operations manager of Playboy's club and hotel division. Lassiter would not cooperate with Al Teller, then the corporate development director. Lassiter, who had been with the Stouffer Foods Corporation prior to joining Playboy, thought he was the logical one to handle the entire venture. His hands were already full trying to revive the steadily sagging profits of the clubs. But he wouldn't budge to put Teller in contact with the proper sources in the food industry. Another venture stalled and died.

Every time Teller tried to get a new venture going, someone gave him a lot of static. Take the time that he was trying to set up the Playboy limousine service. It was Teller's project but another executive had been corresponding with one company for the development of leasing arrangements. At that time the executive was in charge of land development and Teller had taken over his previous job.

Prior to joining Playboy, the executive also had been vice president of marketing with a car rental firm. During the course of his correspondence he was turning down various licensing deals that Teller would have been thrilled to follow up.

Finally, out of frustration, a firm the executive had been turning down called Rosenzweig to find out if there was someone else they could talk to. Rosenzweig told them the man to talk to about licensing was Teller. The first question the company asked Teller was why he had turned down its offers. A bit stunned, he said that he had never heard of the

160

company, much less the correspondence that had been going on for at least eight months. The executive brushed it off, admitting that he may have received a letter or two from them.

Teller was typical of the young executives I tried to bring into the Playboy organization. He is a 28-year-old bachelor with a master's degree from Harvard Business School and a master's in mathematics from Columbia University. When I hired him he was assistant to the president of Columbia Records, a subsidiary of CBS, based in New York City. He drives a Jaguar-XKE and is an avid skier.

Al wears his hair to his shoulders and I never asked him to cut it because I remembered his story of the beard and IBM.

When Al was at Columbia University, he worked three days a week for IBM and when he went for his job interview, he was wearing a three-month beard. He talked first with the man who became his boss and then with that man's superior and both were satisfied that he could do the job. However, there was one thing they weren't happy about—the beard. Al howled when he told me that it was left to the superior "because of his excellent handling of delicate issues" to tell him "quite abruptly" that unless he shaved there was no job.

Well, Al needed the money and he didn't think a three-month beard was such a loss so he shaved, meanwhile promising himself he'd never do that kind of thing again for any job. He worked there for six months and then went off on a ski jaunt to Europe, where he grew another beard. When he returned he got in touch with his IBM boss and said he'd like to go back to work but he'd grown another beard and this time it wasn't coming off. After about a month of waiting while IBM checked it out, he went back to work, jauntily bearded.

"Al, maybe they were afraid you'd get your beard caught in the computer," I suggested.

"Yeah, the card reader," he chuckled. "Anyway, I was the only beard in a building with a thousand people and the whole year I worked there I got funny looks."

Al joined Columbia after graduation from Harvard and

161

another ski vacation in Europe. He'd been there only three months when he was approached by a head hunter and offered a job at Playboy. He was enjoying his work at Columbia and not inclined to leave, but out of curiosity he flew to Chicago and talked with some Playboy executives.

He told me later that the executives "sounded pretty smart for about ten minutes but then in the second ten they repeated what they had said in the first ten. By the time we finished the conversation I realized these guys were all slogans and buzz words. They didn't really have any idea of what they wanted." This was in December 1969.

Asked about salary, Al said he wanted $50,000 plus stock options—this was six months out of Harvard. Playboy, however, had in mind a figure distinctly under $25,000. Teller said he wouldn't consider going to Chicago for less than $30,000. Playboy finally agreed.

Teller didn't really understand what his job was supposed to be so he went off skiing and from France sent a "thanks, but no, thanks" cable.

Several months later I called Teller and asked him why he turned us down.

"Basically, I wasn't too impressed with the people I met," Teller explained. "They didn't know what they wanted, and I thought it was a little too early for me to even consider a switch from Columbia."

"Some dramatic changes have been made here," I said, "and I'd like to talk to you about a more substantial position than you were offered and more money, too." I finally persuaded him to fly out to Chicago and talk it over. That was in April of 1970.

I wanted Teller for a new job I was creating, director of corporate development, a division that was responsible for every new business Playboy got into, every acquisition. When he said he wanted $50,000 and stock options, I offered $40,000 and no stock. He said he'd take $50,000 and no stock and I went to $40,000 and an option on 2,000 shares. It was a deal.

Al told me some time later that he went back to New York

with "sugar plums in my head. It was not so much the money as the excitement over the responsibility. Playboy had the name and I knew it had the money to get into all kinds of great things. And you'd been given the green light to go, we were all going to go. It was a great feeling."

Anyway, Al joined Playboy in late May of 1970 and almost immediately began to feel frustrated because he couldn't find a direction to go in. He couldn't get Preuss to commit himself. Finally he told me, "I'm going to lay out every possible kind of acquisition and new business and read the list off to him and see what his facial expression is. If he smiles I'll put warm, if he frowns, I'll put cold. And then I'll go off in a corner and play with the warm ones."

Well, that meeting was held and afterwards Al asked me what I thought Preuss' facial expressions meant when Al read his list. "Did you think he smiled when I mentioned Artbark Casting?" he asked anxiously. "Or did he frown?"

Preuss was not giving Al the runaround with his noncommitment. He thought of himself as a chief executive officer but in reality it was Hefner, and only Hefner, who could give the nod on acquisitions. I was perhaps at fault, maybe I should have stepped in and given Al more direction than I did, but I had my hands full and running over and felt that since I had given the job to him, I should let him do it.

Al once described to me what happened to him after I left Playboy. First, Preuss called a meeting of senior executives and announced my departure and told them all to report to him from then on. It was the first Al had heard of it.

"I sat there absolutely stunned," he said. "My first rational thought was 'Well, it's all over' but I proceeded as usual. Or tried to. It was like banging my head against the wall. I sent memos trying to set up meetings. I sent proposals. But no response to anything. I tried to talk, to communicate but I was shut up. They wouldn't even talk to me—I had the worst case of corporate bad breath imaginable. I was a real plague case."

Then things got downright ridiculous. In the course of one week three new venture proposals suggested by Playboy executives that crossed Teller's desk were: a barber shop with lady barbers, a Playboy wristwatch with rabbit ears for hands, and the acquisition of a skin-diving shop in a remote corner of California. For a company that's trying to increase its annual revenues significantly above $130 million, you can hardly consider such ventures as blockbusters.

But Teller refused to panic. He tried to approach everything very rationally, regardless of how irrational a proposal seemed. He was, in fact, diplomatic and patient. Take, for example, what he told the executive who proposed the Playboy watch with rabbit-ear hands:

"A watch with hands that are rabbit ears," mused Teller, fighting off laughter. "Well, the hands would look good when it's ten minutes to one because the ears would be up. But at 6:30 you're going to have a most anemic-looking rabbit, with ears down to its gut." Teller was still manfully fighting off laughter.

The executive reflected for a few moments and said: "You know, Al, I never thought of that. You're right. I'm still going to give it some more thought and maybe I can come up with a different design for the watch."

"Yes, you do that," Al said dejectedly.

Teller didn't stay long enough to see an alternate watch design. But he had stuck it out from the beginning of November to the middle of March before giving it up as a bad job.

Some executives preferred to hire subordinates with limited capabilities. The reason was simple enough. The executive didn't have to worry that he might hire a hotshot who might someday replace him. And it bolstered his ego to have mediocre staff around him. Then there were the ego trips—executives who constantly tried to show one another up.

For instance, two executives were separately studying land acquisition sites in Nevada for a Playboy ski resort. One proposed a site that the other had an independent firm denounce, testifying that the site was inaccessible, that it took three hours of driving to reach from the last railroad stop. The other executive's site was turned down as being on the wrong side of the mountain.

164

Another big business decision that centered around Hefner's egomania was the purchase of the Hilton Plaza Hotel in Miami Beach, renamed the Playboy Plaza. Hefner's ego forced him to buy a hotel from Hilton because this was a reaffirmation that Playboy had hit the big time.

Buying a Hilton hotel represented a higher strata of business to him and for all of the man's excellence in business, for all of his achievements, he still feels the stigma of being looked upon as something less than a Conrad Hilton.

He may or may not be right on this, but it certainly is no foundation for buying an enormous hotel that is falling flat on its ass. The Hilton organization had opted out, after fulfilling a two-year management contract on a fee plus profit-sharing basis, because it recognized that Miami Beach was on the downswing and as a result, so was the profit potential.

Other reasons were the high building cost and high mortgage, the huge amount of public space, such as ballrooms, lobbies, halls and other public areas that were not generating profit. The Plaza has 42,000 square feet of such public space and this is an exorbitant nut to bear.

The hotel has proved an expensive ego symbol to Hefner, because in addition to the more than $13 million purchase price and the million spent in refurnishing and remodeling, the hotel had operating losses of $2,161,000 from August, 1970, through June, 1971. During that time, average room occupancy in the peak season months was only 55.2 percent.

Before the purchase, Hefner and Preuss and I, along with Bud Bruder, Arnold Morton, Vic Lownes, Andy Andrin, who is PCI treasurer, and Henri Lorenzi, vice president-director of operations, hotels and clubs, flew to Miami in Hefner's jet. As we circled over Miami Beach, Preuss excitedly pointed out the hotel. It looked impressive because it was night and all the lights were on. Nobody bothered to mention that the lights had not been on for well over six months because with a 10 to 20 percent occupancy rate, who needed spotlights on the hotel at night? Save on electricity.

It was only during the daytime that you could look at the

front of the hotel and see that the mosaic tile was so badly chipped, peeling and falling off that it looked as if the place was in the process of being torn down. It was only upon arriving in the lobby that you could realize the biggest crowd was the group of clerks behind the reservations desk. It's weird to eat meal after meal in a dining room that seats 350 people but has only four tables occupied at the height of the dinner hour.

All these poor prospects were known but nonetheless the purchase was made because of Hefner's desire to be an elite member of the business establishment.

Another loser is the Playboy Towers in Chicago, which also was Hefner's inspiration. He was enamored with the idea of creating a Playboy Center, comprising the office building, the Chicago club and a hotel. This is understandable but in the face of some hefty losses, it's not logical and it's not the basis on which a business should be run.

In the case of the Towers, it was leased, not purchased outright, when the former Knickerbocker Hotel was offered for lease. The agreement was for a net lease to 1987, with renewal options through 2029. The mimimum annual rental is $450,000 plus a percentage rental if specified levels of room, food and beverage sales are reached.

Remodeling and refurnishing cost well over a million dollars and operating losses from November 1970 through June 1971 were $487,000. Occupancy rate during the remodeling was only 49.1 percent of the available rooms.

Hefner got his start peddling bare skin and he's never stopped trying to change that image in the public mind. He's still peddling bare skin and despite his other efforts, it's still the one thing that's paying off for him. Some of the other things may not be outright losers, but they don't produce a big profit.

Anyway, Hefner is still trying to prove that he has class and that's why he financed Roman Polanski and "Macbeth." Culture, man. He was always saying to me and to others, "I have to hit it big, I have to prove that Playboy isn't the sex slush that people think it is."

So he was ready to be hooked when he and Polanski were chatting at a party and Polanski said, "Well, Hef, I hear you're going into movies. Skin flicks?"

"Oh, no," Hefner answered, "we're going to go into good stuff."

And Polanski, seeing that he had a fish, said, "Well, I'm sure you wouldn't be interested in the kind of thing I work on now, because I work on nothing but the greatest dramas of all time. Right now, I have an idea for 'Macbeth.' "

That hit Hefner right in the middle of his ego. This was it, this would prove to the business community that he wasn't just some lucky urchin.

Now, everybody in the movie industry realizes that Shakespeare appeals to a limited audience and yes, there can periodically be a great success if you produce a movie for $200,000 or $300,000 and net $600,000 to a million or more.

Everybody realizes that but Hugh Hefner. No, he budgets more than two million for it and had to ante up another million or so when Polanski went over his budget, as anybody who knew Polanski could have told Hefner he would. The man's a spendthrift.

This was another business decision that Hefner made on his own. He's never made a movie but he's going to prove the movie industry wrong.

Even though he didn't take it, he asked the advice of every executive at Playboy except one, and that was his entertainment director, Ted Rogers. He circulated the script for the movie among the editorial people on the magazine but the man who's supposedly in charge of all Playboy's entertainment ventures wasn't even aware of the project until somebody casually mentioned it to him.

So Rogers, not knowing a thing about it, issued a 'scathing memo that in essence said this was wrong, this was horrible judgment. It should not be done, and that as long as he is entertainment director he will not allow it to happen.

And then, a couple of days later, when Hefner announced that Playboy was going into the movie business and the first vehicle would be "Macbeth," this entertainment director responded that this was a fine, qualified project, that Roman Polanski would bring to "Macbeth" a broad awarness and interest that Shakespearean drama had never had.

So despite the advice of all his executives and his editorial people, Hefner had his way. He made his movie and I understand he plans three more by next year, one of which is "The Naked Ape." But, as Bob Preuss said in a *Forbes* article, "On 'Macbeth' we wanted to go first class to show we were serious. Our next three will cost from $500,000 to $1 million each."

Another business decision I remember is one that Preuss made first and I agreed with later, but it was reversed after I left. I hear Playboy is losing substantial amounts of money with it.

When I hired College Marketing and Research Corp. (CMRC) to assume the responsibilities of what had been the independent representatives contracted directly with Playboy, known collectively as the College Bureau, the first thing I had CMRC do was take an 8,000-person survey on attitudes on the campuses for an editorial feature in the September 1970 issue. The poll was supervised by Mike Kaplan, who was my college marketing director, and myself.

CMRC conducted the poll in two to three weeks, doing a thorough, precise and accurate job of securing, recording and processing opinions. It was a satisfactory relationship, everything was fine.

Under the old system, a College Bureau director at Playboy maintained contact with 600 or so individual representatives around the country. It was inefficient and results were poor. All the reps were doing was buying a few Playboy products a year and passing out some order cards so that some college students would order *Playboy*. The net result was 15,000 subscriptions a year, which would have been sold anyway, and selling about $10,000 worth of Playboy products, cufflinks and such. The reps were paid a percentage of what they sold.

I turned the reps list over to Mark Vittert, who owned

most of CMRC, and hired his organization to take over everything. During the next year, CMRC sold 45,000 subscriptions instead of 15,000; $100,000 worth of Playboy products instead of $10,000 worth; conducted the college poll; and did some advertising promotion work. The reps had the same deal as before, they got a percentage of what they sold. So it was a very good, worthwhile switch, because to run its own College Bureau, it had cost Playboy the salary of a director, $20,000 plus a secretary, another $8,000; overhead, $12,000; travel and entertainment, $5,000 for the year, so that's $45,000, plus accounting and other things that went into it. By using CMRC I got the job done better for less.

Until 1970, the college poll had always been an attitudinal study about sex and that was the whole thing. When I got into it, it was still a questionnaire about sex that Jack Kessie gave to me to turn over to CMRC. I took it to Hefner because I felt that more than at any time in the past, it was sheer narrowmindedness to do another vapid sex survey.

Instead, I thought it ought to go into drugs, crime, civil rights, personal freedoms, news management, Vietnam and so on. But I didn't even have to say all that because no sooner did Hefner look at it than he said, "This is nothing, this is absolutely ridiculous." I told him that was what I'd come to see him about. So the questionnaire was revised to make it more relevant to what was happening on the campus.

When I first started dealing with CMRC, I felt it was a positive organization, that Vittert was a positive person, and I recommended that it be acquired by Playboy. Preuss disagreed. He said it wasn't worth acquiring and we ought to give it a year and see how it worked. Besides that, he said, you weren't really acquiring anything, it was just a group of affiliations with reps that could be broken off at the snap of a finger. So he and I argued but it was no go.

I came to have my doubts about Vittert later. In the end, I agreed with Preuss.

After I left, Preuss and Gutwillig decided that Playboy should acquire it and it was bought for $462,000 in cash and 40,224 shares of Playboy common stock. That was in January 1971 and I am told that what they make during the school year, they are more than losing during the rest of the year because they have such a huge overhead built up.

Also, Vittert quit three weeks after the sale, ostensibly because his mother was sick. That's the reason he gave Playboy. He must have had happy hysterics as he walked away with that chunk of Playboy's greenbacks.

The '71 college poll was taken by an outside research organization and what I conclude is that the college marketing division is not functioning well and could not satisfactorily handle the project as it had the previous year.

Chapter 14
Win Some — Lose Some

Hefner's feelings about the losses at the Playboy Clubs are that they are due totally to mismanagement, because certainly each of the cities in which the clubs are located can successfully support one.

He personally feels the clubs are superior in concept, decor, service and food. Although Hefner seems gradually to be realizing that there isn't a great future for the clubs, I don't think he has honestly recognized that they are outdated in the most important ingredient of all, their desirability to the public.

The reason he doesn't recognize it is that when he goes to a club, it is with forewarning enough that the exterior of the club may be repainted only hours before he gets there so that it gives him a good impression. The service, for him, is impeccable and surrounding him are the most beautiful Bunnies they can find. The general manager escorts him to the choicest table and special entertainment is presented, so he naturally thinks the clubs are neat. That evening, for him, they are. But that has absolutely nothing to do with the day-to-day operations. The next day the club goes back to being the same dreary place it was the day before.

Playboy Enterprises, Inc., which has seventeen of these profit-drainers, is in a box, according to its legal beagles. Their opinion is that Playboy has locked itself into a situation that requires maintenance of the clubs, profitable or not. Legal counsel says keys were sold on the basis of there being a club in a given city, or location that the keyholder might travel to, and that if that club fails, then Playboy faces making refunds to every keyholder in that city or to everyone who claims that he joined on the basis of there being a club located in a certain city. It's that legal opinion that keeps a club in operation at a site where it's losing a half-million dollars a year, such as Los Angeles; $400,000 a year in Montreal; $300,000 in Detroit, and so on.

The obvious answer is, why not reduce the overhead and minimize the losses? That is a hard decision for a business enterprise to make. It's difficult for any company to admit publicly that it's just barely keeping its doors open.

And yet, by going public, Playboy Enterprises now faces the other side of the situation because a stockholder has the right to ask why his company is losing money; why it doesn't close that gap; he has the right to point out that it's costing him dollars because Playboy keeps unprofitable clubs open.

These unpalatable circumstances are why Playboy is leaning more and more toward resort hotels and other enterprises in its corporate development.

It now has four resort hotels, located in Lake Geneva, Wisconsin; Miami Beach, Florida; Jamaica, West Indies, and Great Gorge, New Jersey, which is the largest of the four. In addition, it leases the Playboy Towers in Chicago. As of the end of the last fiscal year, June 30, 1971, the company had a net investment in land, buildings and furnishings of $7,036,000 for all Playboy Clubs and $55,534,000 for the hotels.

Entry to Playboy Clubs was at one time restricted to keyholders and their guests but a number are now open to the public in the sense that guests in the hotels are given

172

guest club keys to be used during their stay.

If the hotels sang the blues because of opening operational losses, the clubs are in real trouble. For one thing, many of them are in undesirable downtown locations, and for another, a large number of blacks are frequenting the clubs. Some executives maintain that this has discouraged the attendance of white patrons.

The Playboy Club-Hotel of Lake Geneva not only takes business away from the Chicago club but is also popular with the black people. In addition, it has had trouble attracting repeat groups because of ineptitude in running the place.

The large numbers of blacks at the clubs and hotels drove one top club executive crazy. He'd say, "Why do these fucking niggers go to the Lake Geneva hotel? Don't they have any place else to go?" Things like that, three, four, seven times a day. He was freaking out because he was getting serious complaints from a lot of white people. He tried to discourage blacks from frequenting the club, but he was unsuccessful.

Playboy claims Lake Geneva is for the first time showing a profit. I don't know how that accounting is done. It was losing vast amounts of money throughout my time at Playboy. And occupancy has been relatively stable, climbing slightly to 61.4 percent in fiscal 1971 from 59.5 percent in fiscal 1970 and 59 percent in fiscal 1969. The average cost of a room has declined to $29.82 (1971) from $30.44 (1970) and $29.99 (1969).

I seriously question that the Lake Geneva operation is a money-making proposition now for this reason: Advertising in all Chicago newspapers as often as three or four times a week offers package deals to Lake Geneva—including a Playboy Club key—for $39 a person, modified American plan. This indicates to me that they are having a great deal of difficulty in selling Playboy keys and that business is poor. You do not advertise deals like that if business is good, you stop advertising except for minimal space ads to keep your name before the public. Playboy also says that its Jamaica hotel in Ocho Ricos is profitable. Acquired in January 1964, the 200-room facility has had a steady decline in occupancy for the past three fiscal years, dropping to 65.6 percent in 1971 from 79.8 percent in 1970 and 84.2 percent in 1969.

Key sales have been declining since 1967, when 103,713 were sold, to 1971's 76,677. Total keys outstanding as of July 28, 1971, were 928,000.

As with key sales, year by year keyholder studies have recorded increasing disenchantment. The keyholders have become more and more disgruntled with the clubs. In the last study that was done while I was there, I recall that the biggest criticisms were of service, nothing to do at the club, poor entertainment, and unappealing food. This was a survey made by Dr. Charles King of Purdue University, whom I had commissioned for a poll of consumer attitudes toward Playboy.

The individual responsible for lining up talent at the clubs was fired last year, allegedly for being on the take. A long-time employee of Playboy Clubs International, it was reported that his kickback from one talent agency alone exceeded $25,000 a year. When he was fired, he was told that he was being banned from the Playboy Mansion, that Hefner never wanted him there again. End of drama.

The talent for the hotels was handled by a capable, attractive young lady named Arlyne Rothberg, who left Playboy last October when she was married to a young actor, Bill Gerber. Arlyne was responsible for getting some top talent into the hotels, like Sonny and Cher, Ann-Margret, Marlene Dietrich, Phyllis Diller, and people like that.

How the club locations are picked gives an insight into Playboy operations. In Los Angeles it's on the Strip, on Sunset Boulevard, because in Hefner's view, he being rooted in the '50s, Sunset is the Mecca of Los Angeles. Today it is a tired, dreary street where nothing is happening. Wherever it is happening, it isn't there. But it was romantic to Hefner, so that's where the club is located.

The Detroit club is in a slum area near downtown Detroit. It's not near the new convention center or the nice part of the city; instead it's on a street equivalent to West Madison in

Chicago. The reason it's there is that the original franchise holder owned that piece of property through another company and he was able to rake in a very handsome amount because Playboy shared the purchase price of the land. It was a deal to get something going for himself.

In Montreal it was a similar situation. The land was owned by Tony Roma, who became the franchise holder. New York has a good site, but some of the others are abominable. It's in a terrible location in Cincinnati, Atlanta, and Miami, where it really should have been located in Miami Beach.

When Arnold Morton took over planning and development of the club-hotel division, he hired Bill Lassiter as operations director.

Lassiter had been with the Ogden Corp., the Stouffer organization, the Greyhound Corp., and several others and he is a prime example of what happens at Playboy. Once, when my wife and I went out to dinner with him, he showed us his clip necktie, which he wore because his elbow wouldn't bend—he demonstrated that, too. But it was when he stuck out his tongue to show us how he had bitten part of it off in an auto accident that I said to myself, what am I doing here?

Anyway, when I asked what his background was and how long he had been in this end of the business he said, "Young man, let me tell you something, I put Vernon Stouffer on the map." And other things like that. He left in January 1971, about ten months after he was hired. He was replaced by Henri Lorenzi, who was previously employed by the Lowe's Corp. as managing director of the Americana Hotel in San Juan, Puerto Rico.

There was one club executive who preferred using psychology to keep the clubs in shape. When a club stank of garbage in the alley, and the paint was peeling off the front of the building, and a step was broken going from the first to the second floor, instead of hauling away the garbage, painting the building, and fixing the stair, he'd assemble a course in group dynamics and request that everybody at the club go through an encounter session so that they would understand the reason why things weren't right.

175

I saw all this when I visited the New Orleans Club. It was a mess. Back in Chicago, I said, "Bill, have you been to New Orleans?"

"No I haven't," he said, "but I've had the manager up here and he's working out nicely."

"My ass, he's working out nicely," I told him, "that club stinks, literally and figuratively, I can't say anything good about it," and I rattled off the problems, "for Christ's sake, I've never seen such a shambles."

"Steve," he said, "I can't go down there myself and clean the floors and paint the building. You have to get people to want to take pride in themselves."

"Paint the building," I said, "that's how you're going to get customers. You aren't going to get customers by this jerk down there taking pride in himself. You're only going to get customers if the building is painted, if the place doesn't stink of garbage, if the food is decent. They serve shrimp creole six days a week in that stupid club and every hamburger stand in New Orleans serves shrimp creole six days a week. Have them serve something from another part of the country. Get some entertainment in there, clean up the place, fix the stairs."

"No, no," he said, "it'll take a little longer my way but it'll be deeper-seated. These people will have pride in themselves and therefore they'll do well."

"That's a lot of nonsense," I said. And it is.

But maybe Spectorsky should have had the last word on the clubs, because of what he said in an interview that appeared in *Forbes* in March 1971. It was probably the first time that a senior officer of Playboy had publicly knocked the clubs. He said:

"The decor seems dated. The Bunny costume is dated and it is ammunition for those who say we treat women as objects. The cuisine is less than first-rate. Also, the clubs' strong appeal to the middle-aged businessman is that he can come on horny without having to perform, and the reason his wife likes the clubs—and wives do—is that she can boss around a much prettier girl (the Bunny waitress)." I wonder what Morton said about Spec's comment?

Forbes went on to conclude: "Spectorsky's analysis helps explain why it has become increasingly difficult to sell club membership keys while *Playboy's* readership has soared."

The average club patron doesn't even read *Playboy*. He is 38 years old, making him about ten years older than the average *Playboy* reader.

Losing propositions, however, are not new to Hefner. In August 1961, he launched a semi-monthly magazine called *Show Business Illustrated*, devoted to covering the entertainment world. It was to be both reporter and critic of radio, TV, movies and records. The magazine consisted of four main sections: (1) the news and review section provided general coverage of the entertainment field . . . (2) the second section included a listing and rating of movies, plays, TV programs, records and concerts . . . (3) the third was composed of nonfiction stories or articles by known writers . . . (4) the fourth was the photographic material that accompanied the features and stories. It was all seasoned with a sprinkling of humor.

The first edition of *SBI* went on sale August 23, 1961. Its newsstand price of fifty cents made it the most expensive semi-monthly at that time. An introductory subscription offered twelve issues for $4. The regular subscription price was twenty-five issues for $8.50

Hefner hired Frank Gibney as *SBI's* editorial director. Gibney's credentials were quite impressive. An author of several books, he had formerly been with *Life, Time* and *Newsweek* magazines. Because of its peg on current events, Hefner aspired to eventually turn *SBI* into a weekly publication.

But those aspirations never materialized because *SBI* folded after eight months. The magazine found less than the anticipated acceptance. Hefner had promised advertisers a circulation base of 350,000, but only 200,000 copies were being sold.

The magazines' backlog of manuscripts and its advertising contracts and subscription list were sold to *SBI's* chief competitor at that time, *Show* magazine, for $250,000. It was hardly enough, however, to lighten the $1.5 million loss *SBI* sustained in its brief life. *Show,* which was launched at the same time as *SBI,* is still being published by Huntington Hartford, an heir to the Great Atlantic & Pacific Tea Co. fortune.

Hefner blamed *SBI's* demise on himself, saying that he neglected to give the magazine enough attention in its initial stages. (Closing date for the first issue of *SBI* was only three months after it had assembled its editorial staff. Most magazines take at least a year in the planning before they are introduced.) Gibney, who became publisher of *Show,* didn't look at *SBI's* failure the way Hefner did:

"I wanted to intellectualize *SBI.* Hefner wanted to use his *Playboy* techniques and make everything breathless. The two concepts just didn't go together," Gibney told *The Wall Street Journal* in 1962. He went on to say that "most of the first issue I wouldn't have put in any magazine. Everyone agreed each succeeding issue got better but the question was how fast."

Playboy Tours, a travel organization, was set up in 1960 to conduct guided tours through Europe, Jamaica, Hawaii and Mexico. The purpose of this venture was to show the travel industry that Playboy was an effective medium for travel advertising. In 1961 the operation was bringing in only 25 percent of its anticipated volume. Ad revenue from the travel industry was trickling in at the rate of about $4,400 a month. By 1962, Playboy tours stopped going anywhere.

While *SBI* didn't mean a financial crisis for Hefner, it did crimp his plans to expand in the publishing field.

But *Show Business Illustrated* wasn't the first setback Hefner experienced in publishing. In 1956 he started *Trump,* a monthly magazine that satirized radio and TV. Many of the magazines' key people had been previously associated with MAD comics. *Trump* suspended publication after about a year because, as a Playboy executive later explained, there was a lack of control over the New York operation.

When *SBI* folded, Hefner considered going back into television, a media in which he had previously bombed. His first try at TV was in 1959 with "Playboy's Penthouse," a series he hosted. The show combined talk, entertainment, pretty girls and celebrities in a party atmosphere. It was sold by two independent distributors to individual TV stations around the country. Few stations, however, were willing to buy Hefner's visual rendering—in living black and white—of how the beautiful people live the good life. In July 1961, only twenty out of five hundred and eighty TV stations in the U.S. carried the show. The thirty-seven hours of programming that had been aired during 1959-60 resulted in a net loss of $496,000. The show was dropped sometime in 1961.

Hefner tried TV a second time with his "Playboy After Dark" series, which began airing in 1969. Again, he tried to sell an eyeful of the good life—this time in living color—through syndication. Again, there were few buyers. The show was discontinued in 1971. It was a losing proposition, accounting for a major portion of the $1,217,000 loss Playboy suffered in fiscal 1970 in its "Other Businesses" operations (movie production, book club, paperback books, limousine service, model agency, movie theater operation, and a variety of consumer products).

Ventures that Playboy is progressing on include a hardcover book club and a music publishing and record production business. The book club, as of June 30, 1971, had cost the company a net investment of approximately $500,000 in operations that had a net operating loss of $275,000 in fiscal 1971. As might be expected, the books offered are catholic in scope—anything from sex to wines to jokes to violence. One was described as an "exotic, erotic adventure novel," for instance, and another as "sex and violence in Paris." But there are serious books, too, novels and non-fiction, and sports and political selections.

Playboy's involvement in movie-making and the musical world inspired Hefner's purchase of the Playboy Mansion West, which cost $1.5 million. He expects to live there about six months out of the year. The music division—start-up costs estimated at $500,000—is based in Los Angeles, as is the movie project, which will be in conjunction with such well-established companies as Columbia, Universal and 20th Century Fox.

A Playboy casino afloat is another new venture. It was installed on a Greek cruise ship and plans are for six more if that one pays off. A resort and casino is in the works for Morocco, outside Tangiers on the Mediterranean.

A gaming and liquor license has been obtained for a company in Manchester, England, in which Playboy Club of London Ltd., a wholly-owned subsidiary, owns an 80 percent stock interest, with a deferred option to acquire the remaining 20 percent. Playboy Club of London has acquired a leasehold interest in some premises in Manchester and intends to establish a gaming club under its supervision. Costs of remodeling and furnishing and the pre-opening expenses are expected to reach about $500,000.

Another foreign development is in the Costa del Sol region of Spain. About two hundred and seventy-five acres of land will be used for a resort and hotel complex. The total purchase price is $950,000, of which about $400,000 has been paid. If no further payments are made, Playboy Enterprises will be entitled to a proportion of the total land covered by the contract, based upon payments already made.

There also has been talk about opening "mini-clubs" around the country. They would be small restaurant bars staffed by Bunnies, of course, but without entertainment facilities. Such clubs are likely to become a part of the singles apartment complexes Playboy has been negotiating to have built by Levitt & Sons, the creators of sprawling suburban developments known as Levittowns. Los Angeles and Hollywood, Florida, are proposed sites for the singles' apartments, the first of which will have about 250 units.

All these various projects mean hefty start-up costs and initially, probable losses. But the profit potential, Hefner feels, is well worth the risk. And Playboy can still afford to take risks.

Despite all its setbacks, Playboy Enterprises, Inc., has been a continuous money-maker, mainly because of its flagship—*Playboy* magazine. The magazine's revenues, which in fiscal

1971 rose to $73.8 million from $68 million the previous year, accounted for more than half of the company's overall revenue. Total corporate revenue in 1971 was $131.5 million compared with $119.6 million in fiscal 1970. The magazine's profits also account for most of the overall profits as well. *Playboy's* 1971 pretax profits climbed to $16.8 million from $15.6 million. The increase helped boost Playboy Enterprises' net income to about $9.2 million, or $1.07 a share, from $8.3 million, or 95 cents a share, the year before.

The seventeen Playboy key clubs posted a pretax profit of $3.17 million in fiscal 1971, down slightly from $3.39 million in fiscal 1970. The clubs' revenues also declined to $29 million from $30.6 million.

Playboy's hotel operations had a pretax loss of $1.7 million in fiscal 1971, compared with a pretax profit of $39,000 in the prior year. The loss resulted despite an increase in hotel revenues to $18.5 million from $12.6 million. Last September Playboy said it may incur further operating losses at its Miami Beach and Chicago hotels. It also anticipates "substantial operating losses" at its Great Gorge resort-hotel, an adult Disneyland located on 567 acres in northern New Jersey, about fifty miles from downtown New York City. Initially, Playboy said the cost of this 674-room facility, which opened last February, would be about $21 million. But it has since reported a revised cost of $29.5 million, noting that the revised figure "may be increased by changes to current design or other construction plans." If I know Playboy, when everything is totaled, that revised figure will have been revised.

Building Great Gorge saddled Playboy with a sizable debt, which amounted to nearly $20.5 million on September 1, 1971.

In fact, most of the $27.25 million Playboy intended to get from the sale of 1,159,562 shares of Playboy common stock last November will go to pay off debts incurred in the construction of Great Gorge. The company put up 600,000 shares and the rest came from individual stockholders. The number of shares in the offering comprised about 12 percent of the company's 9,344,617 outstanding common shares. The value of the offering was based on the opening price of $23.50 a share.

It was the first time Playboy shares had been offered to the public. (A public offering of 15 percent ownership in Playboy Clubs International was set for the winter of 1962, but the stock market plummeted that year, dashing Playboy's hopes of a successful offering. So the plans were dropped.) Until the November stock offering, Playboy had relied mainly on internally generated funds and bank loans to finance its various ventures.

When Playboy went public, Hefner became one of the richest self-made men in the country. The paper worth of his holdings amounted to about $157 million. Of the 1,159,562 shares to be sold, 300,000 shares (worth more than $7 million before taxes) came from Hefner's own portfolio. He still retained 6,700,000 shares, or 71.9 percent of the outstanding total. Each Playboy share pays an annual dividend of 11-3/7 cents on each share. It provides Hefner with a tidy $800,000 a year coupled with his annual salary of $303,847. Accumulated in his profit-sharing account is another $372,924.

Other individual shareholders who sold shares included Glenn Hefner, 105,000, worth nearly $2.5 million; Art Paul, 90,000, worth $2.1 million; Preuss, 10,000, worth $235,000.

Preuss, along with the other Playboy officers and directors, has options to buy additional stock at bargain basement prices. Preuss, for example, has an option expiring August 28, 1972, to buy another 21,000 shares at $6.86 a share. I had an option on 17,000 shares at about $15 a share, but I never exercised it. The option was spread over five years. I could have bought as much as 20 percent of the 17,000 shares in each of the five years, or I could have bought all of them in the fifth year. Considering what the stock sold for when Playboy went public—$23.50 a share—I wish I had.

Chapter 15
What's In A *Playboy*?

What does *Playboy* magazine do besides bring some level of entertainment to the consumer? Perhaps that's enough. Maybe there should be no other purpose to many things. Perhaps comedian Flip Wilson should have no other function and that's fine, because Flip Wilson says he is there to entertain.

But Playboy Enterprises says something quite different. It says through publicity and through its foundation, its editorial product, in speeches by its executives that it is something vastly above and beyond entertainment.

Playboy magazine claims it is a vehicle bringing to the populace a point of view, a statement about how this ought to be and can be a better world. And it bases this claim upon its involvement with prison reform, the rights of minorities, the effort to change outdated, illogical and irrational legislation having to do with sexual mores, and so on.

And yet it begs the question of how it is most at fault with its consumer public—and that is by playing on the public's tremendous weakness in not being able to judge the difference between a person and a thing. *Playboy* attempts to substitute a thing for a person, like a number for a name.

Is *Playboy* right in cultivating a readership that accepts women as objects? Is it right or valid or honest in cultivating a readership that will not accept the product unless it has its monthly dosage of nude photography? (When it isn't supplied, there is a definite increase in subscription cancellations, a definite decrease in new subscription results from ads and coupons appearing in that issue.) Is *Playboy* right when it says it is a proponent of women's lib and yet continues to maintain an artificial attitude toward the recognition of women as something other than as an article of form?

I remember something *Business Week* magazine published about *Playboy* in June 1969. It quoted a college activist as saying, "*Playboy* is practically the voice of the establishment. Young guys today are interested in more than cars and hi-fi sets and carefully posed pictures of balloon-bosomed Bunnies." In response to that, Spectorsky said, "*Playboy* is neither establishment nor dissident—it is a mediator." A mediator of what? Between generations, between activists and the establishment, a mediator of dress codes, of philosophies?

I don't believe Spectorsky's statement. I believe, instead, that *Playboy* is a very comfortable old-shoe habit that, if and when its readers examine its true value to them, will be discarded. They will say, "I've outgrown *Playboy*. It meant something to me when I was 13 and 15 and 17 and 19, but it no longer means that to me. I don't need it. It doesn't fill a void in my life or in my life style or in my reading habits."

Playboy is now eighteen years old, which is not a short time for a magazine, but within the broader sphere of a lifetime it isn't a very long period. By the second half of the 1950s, when it started to gain wider circulation, it was truly an innovative, interesting and rewarding publication. It brought sex out of the furtive and dusty corner it had thus far occupied within the magazine world, like the *Police Gazette*. It satisfied other needs, that is, the need to know more about the life style towards which its readership could hope to direct itself. It taught readers about stereo and camera equipment and luxury items that were of interest and benefit to consumers. It filled a void by bringing to the magazine public fiction and non-fiction articles that were of very real value.

But over the last ten-year period, how has it changed? It hasn't. It has the same art direction, typography, pace, cartoonists—every aspect of the publication is virtually identical with what it was ten or fifteen years ago. This is neither good nor desirable, because too many conditions in the country and the world have changed in that period.

Today, the situation has altered in two ways. Number one, there are other magazines that bring to the public the same ingredients that *Playboy* brings. There are magazines such as *Penthouse* and *Esquire,* which has staged a great revival. Furthermore, the magazine-buying public, as everyone in the industry recognizes, has become more appreciative of special interest publications and while *Playboy* began as a special interest publication of sorts—call it a life-style magazine—it no longer is that. By the nature of its tremendous audience growth, it has had to broaden itself in its editorial format, keeping it from in-depth coverage of any one subject to the satisfaction of readers interested in a specific topic.

It cannot do for stereo equipment what *Hi-Fi Stereo Review* can do; for photographic equipment and enjoyment what *Pop Photo* or *Modern Photo* can; for travel what any of a half-dozen different magazines can; or for political coverage, or fiction and so on down the line.

Number two, perhaps more significantly, more and more people daily become more concerned about what affects not only them but those around them. In what generation or what years has there ever been such public turmoil over ecology, or racial relationships, or the idiocy of undeclared war? Over the equality of not only racial minorities but other real or imagined minorities, such as women, ethnic groups? Over the management of our media by the government? And what about the very striking concern that the government has not taken the first step toward maintaining a credible posture with the public?

Today the void or gap filled by *Playboy* means very little. But in the late 1950s and early 1960s *Playboy* developed as its audience core a group of people, many of whom are still within that core. It's a big, big segment to whom *Playboy* is a very real habit. Now, with that core audience arriving at the age that it finally realizes that *Playboy* doesn't mean much to it any more, there will be a noticeable drop-off in circulation. It hasn't happened yet, however. It has to happen because *Playboy's* appeal is not to an older group, but to a younger one whose thoughts are taken up with things other than the superfluous fluff that Playboy is delivering every month.

This does not prognosticate in any way the demise of *Playboy*. God love Hefner, the man has been able to do remarkable things. He's become a multi-millionaire following his emotions and his judgments. This merely says that it will be more and more difficult for the magazine to satisfy its audience. Too many things have changed and *Playboy* magazine is not one of them.

Many people have for years thought of Hefner as being the instigator of evolutionary change regarding pornography and censorship, but Hefner has always been a victim of circumstances, thrust into that role after he first implemented the idea in 1953, when he took sex out of the publication sewers and slicked it up for the masses.

And yet since then, his own awareness of the public's tastes and standards has been further and further from being on target.

Now let's jump from 1953, when he for the first time unveiled the female body in a publication in a tasteful, decorous manner, to 1970 when he verbally assaulted Robert Guccione, the publisher of *Penthouse*, for publishing cheap pornography.

The specific examples he cited at a meeting with Preuss, Rosenzweig and me were that in every single pictorial spread, the two things that Guccione emphasized were pubic hair and the girls fondling their own breasts. Hefner called this cheap pornographic crap. The third thing he mentioned was poor photography, grainy and seamy-looking.

186

(Yet by the August 1971 issue of *Playboy*, very distinctly, very noticeably grainy photography depicted pubic hair and girls fondling their breasts.)

Hefner started this whole thing of challenging the public's and the censor's views on what really is and is not pornography. That was a fantastic thing in the 1950s but by 1970 he had lost track of what was happening in regard to the liberalism the public was showing. He was completely unaware that pubic hair no longer meant obscenity, that a girl with her hands on her breasts was not necessarily pornographic, because she might not be fondling them, but merely resting her hands across them.

Several of the staff tried to tell Hefner but at the time he wouldn't listen. Jack Kessie was a strong proponent for more open photography. Mike Demarest was quite strong on liberalizing it. Art Paul spoke up and so did Tajiri, who also spoke for several of his photographers.

A staff photographer and I discussed it. He felt he was going to be looking elsewhere for a job because there was such heavy retouching on everything he did that it rarely bore resemblance to what he had shot originally.

All of these people together may have finally convinced Hefner that there should be some liberalization of the principles he had maintained until then.

You might say that after eighteen years, Playboy has finally entered puberty. Perhaps L. E. Sissman, writing on "The Business of Sex" in the August 1971 issue of *Atlantic Monthly*, summed up *Playboy's* role as well as anybody:

"The first step of this highly commercialized (though not conspiratorial) brainwashing process occurs when we have our sexual expectations raised for us by contact with some magazine or book or movie. *Playboy* is the proto-villain in all of this, the first mass pusher of the drug of sex to the sensually disadvantaged of all ages, the first mass marketer of measured doses of addictive sexual sensation, as Walt Disney was the first mass marketer of measured doses of addictive cruelty.

"Like Disney, *Playboy* went about its dirty work of prettifying, trivializing, and making palatably cute (for example, 'Bunny' for paid temptress) a part of the human condition within certain well-defined limits of decency.

"Thus it is not alone because of postal regulations that *Playboy* has not, until very recently (and then very timidly), admitted pictorially the existence of pubic hair; it is also partly because *Playboy* needs desperately to be accepted by reader and advertiser alike as an unsubversive, overground publication that is part of the system, and partly because *Playboy's* sick male-chauvinist philosophy cannot admit the existence of a woman's sexual power, as signified visibly by pubic hair. In fact, *Playboy's* central marketing strategy is to sell fantasies of women as powerless, grateful sexual slaves to men who have found women far otherwise—strong, demanding, and frightening—in real life.

"But if *Playboy* confines itself to selling sanitized masturbatory fantasies, other magazines, books, and movies—for a variety of motives, ranging from literary integrity to naked greed—do not. Perceiving our growing permissiveness, they have rushed to fill the vacuum with millions of feet and words of increasingly frank sexual portrayal."

Hefner often asked me for my views on the editorial content of *Playboy* magazine, on covers, layouts and pacing.

I became sort of an arbiter of good taste to him because of one particular article, a pictorial satire showing various forms of pot parties. It came off in such a lewd, pornographic fashion that when he showed me the transparencies I was really astounded that Kessie and Nat Lehrman had gone along with it. There were some very raunchy photographs depicting gang-bangs and spreadeagle crotch shots, and one of a marijuana joint protruding from the vagina of one of the girls.

It was so raw—and it was at the press proof stage when Hefner showed it to me and asked for my opinion. I was tempted, slightly, not to comment because this was in the summer of 1970 and I had already become the scourge of the Playboy Building because I'd fired a lot of people. It would have been an easy thing not to involve myself, so as not to have to fight off the pagan horde from the editorial department. And yet how could I not comment, how could I help but be strongly repelled by this lewd trash?

I called it an atrocity, among other things, and Hefner only had to hear the words and he said, "That's exactly what I felt. However, I thought perhaps I was becoming squeamish and I'm glad to hear you confirm my suspicions."

In any case, I don't really think *Playboy* would have run that spread. I think Hefner would have asked the same question of some of his editorial staff, Spectorsky, perhaps Preuss, whom he periodically consulted on editorial matters; I think he would have rechecked with Kessie and Lehrman and that at least one of them, probably all of them, would have detected his attitude from the outset and quickly gone along with him.

There had been other occasions when he asked my opinion. Once was on a houseboat article done in Florida. It was a service feature—an editorial spread about a product or a group or category of products or services—and he consulted me on such articles as how to take a vacation in Aspen or on stereo equipment coverage, gifts for Dad to grab, a Christmas gift spread, things like that.

On the gift spread, he asked whether I felt the gifts actually were unusual and interesting and not simply a rehash of what everybody had already done. I told him yes, it was a rehash, but it was too late to do anything about it.

One long, intense discussion that lasted perhaps four or five hours had to do with the photographic presentation of nudes. Hefner had been ambivalent in his feelings about the nude photography for a long time. He'd criticize it caustically one day and then sound its praises the next.

I thought at the time that he was caught in a dilemma: On the one hand he questioned the competence of the photographic department, feeling it lacked the breadth, the scope, the depth that *Playboy* needed. And opposing this, he'd think, "We've done it this way for years, why should I mess with a known successful formula?"

The frosting on Playboy's cake is that the magazine's mail

subscriptions and single copy sales pay production costs almost entirely, leaving lusty advertising revenues as "found" money, to be lavishly used in financing new ventures.

It is no cause for wonder, then, that each issue of the magazine is babied from inception to after the press run starts—literally. Hefner sees the first few copies off the press and the final run is not started until he approves the quality of the printing. That can take several days.

I knew, of course, that *Playboy* magazine was fantastically successful and I decided to dig into every aspect of its operation until I understood the "how" and could then, perhaps, deduce the "why" of its success. What with a big, new job, and then, very shortly, a bigger, newer job, I had little time to devote to research but I put that time to good usage in conversations with people such as Spectorsky (editorial), Lederer (advertising) and Mastro (production), as well as Alvin Wiemold and Vincent Thompson (circulation). Bob Preuss was a big source of information, too, as business manager.

Checking into overall costs, I found that just to produce and circulate the magazine ran up a bill of about $32 million per year. The magazine spends $1.5 million a year for articles, photographs and fiction purchased from outside; $2.5 million for staff departments; $26 million for paper and printing; $1.75 million for newsstand distribution. Its total shipping costs, including postage, in connection with magazine sales, including subscriptions, amounted to approximately $3,769,000 in fiscal 1971. Rises in postal rates are expected to increase that by $2 million over the next five years.

The content of the magazine can be roughly divided into four parts: fiction, 10 percent; nonfiction, 20 percent; cartoons and photography, 30 percent, and miscellaneous, 7 percent.

Fictional material is submitted by professional authors through their agents and accounts for 99 percent of the fiction used; the other one percent is picked out of a "slush pile," composed of manuscripts submitted directly by amateur writers. About 500 of these are received each week and 100 from agents. All are read by staff members.

Nonfiction articles can be classified as informative, such as one by J. Paul Getty, who is designated as business and finance on the masthead, or other well-known personalities. Informative articles are contracted for with authors who agree to write a definite number each year. Individual viewpoint material originates either from an outsider who sells his idea to the editors, or with an insider's idea which is contracted to an author by the magazine.

While early issues ran reprints, such as Sherlock Holmes stories and Ray Bradbury's science fiction, along with cartoons and stock pictures of girls, today the magazine is a top market for freelancers. It gets first crack at anything Bradbury writes, for instance, and has similar deals with other top authors. It buys new material from such "names" as Truman Capote, Vladimir Nabokov, Justice William O. Douglas and Irvin Shaw.

It's easy to see why Playboy attracts the best of the crop. It pays the top dollar. The lead story or article each month is worth a minimum of $3,000; other stories and articles, $1,500, and for a one-page feature or fictional short-short, the fee is $600. Novelettes and new book excerpts or condensations can bring from $15,000 to $25,000. And any member of the staff whose literary effort is accepted receives the same payment as an outsider.

As with fiction, the great majority of the cartoons come from outside, either contracted for or from freelancers. Two associate editors screen those and the final choices are made by the entire editorial staff.

That Hefner values his contributing authors was underlined by a "happening" he dreamed up in 1971—the Playboy International Writers' Convocation in October, a three-day meeting with a three-fold mission.

As he greeted the assembled sixty-five "name" writers, all contributors in the last ten years, Hefner explained that the object of the session was to "have a good time, to explore ways in which we and our contributors can work more fruitfully together and to learn what you think of *Playboy*."

All the ingredients were present for a good time and a rewarding session—those who accepted the invitation were flown to Chicago from wherever in the world they were; they were housed in the Playboy Towers; their rooms were supplied with such niceties as liquor, fruit and cheeses and the estimated $50,000 to $100,000 tab for all this was picked up by *Playboy*. No Bunnies were in evidence.

But despite all those brilliant brains overflowing the landscape, the whole affair seems to have come off in a downbeat way. The seminars, on such topics as "Beyond Journalism," "The New Urban Life Style," and "The Future of Sex," never really got off the ground, according to reports from some of those attending. Dull, some said dully after long, boring panel sessions.

The literary set was represented by such notables as George Axelrod, John Cheever, James Dickey, Jules Feiffer, Bruce Jay Friedman, Richard Hooker, Sean O'Faolain and Kenneth Tynan. And there were the journalists, Tom Wicker, David Halberstram, Murray Kempton, Art Buchwald, Gary Wills, Larry L. King, Nicholas von Hoffman, Gay Talese and Studs Terkel. Economist John Kenneth Galbraith and historian Arthur Schlesinger Jr. were among the academics and Mary Calderone and William Masters of Masters and Johnson were just two of the eminent sexologists in attendance.

Perhaps it was a case of too many with too much to offer, like a too-rich dessert after a too-heavy dinner. In any case, it was not the scintillating gathering visualized by Hefner.

So the answer to the question of what the convocation accomplished, except more publicity for *Playboy*, may not appear for some time, or never, although it is hard to believe that such creative talent and intellect could foregather under the same roof and produce nothing tangible, not even opinions.

Almost everything that happens in the publishing field seems to work out as a plus for *Playboy*. The regrettable demise of the *Saturday Evening Post* and *Look*, both of which were lucrative outlets for freelancers, left *Playboy* and

Esquire in a class by themselves. (*Life* and *National Geographic* pay well, too, but accept far fewer freelance pieces.)

But one of the most popular and widely read features in the magazine is composed of neither professional nor amateur output. It's The Playboy Advisor and might be described as a male Ann Landers except that the Advisor gets asked questions that most advice columnists could never get past the editors. But not all of the inquiries have to do with sex. A query about high and low efficiency speakers may be sandwiched between an agonized plea from a man who wants to marry a woman but not her four children, and a girl who wants to lose her virginity but hasn't managed to accomplish it in six tries.

Or conversely, a sad tale of a bed joke that went wrong—or came to the inevitable conclusion, depending on the viewpoint—may be preceded by a question of octane content of gasolines for sports cars and followed by a discussion of food.

The variety could never be arrived at in any other form and that's why it is so readable; besides which it is often good for a laugh. In addition, it performs a service for people like the left-handed reader who had heard there were left-handed playing cards and wanted to know if it was a put-on or were they for real. He was told where he could get them and other items made strictly for southpaws.

Or the teenager who said that he and his girl wanted to share pre-marital sex but had been so strictly raised that they knew nothing about it and wanted to know where to go for advice. The Advisor told them to read *Sex Before Marriage* by Dr. Eleanor Hamilton.

That the Advisor takes his responsibilities seriously is evident in the answers he gives. There are no cheap quips but when there is room for humor, he doesn't miss that, either. For instance, a man asked what to do to keep his neighbor's friendship after a strip poker game progressed to a kissing and caressing game that ended with his making love to his friendly neighbor's wife. The friendly neighbor was enraged and ordered him and his wife to leave. The man didn't think an

193

apology was due. The Advisor told him that his actions couldn't be considered unusual in view of the game they were playing but that it wouldn't hurt to offer an apology if he wished to retain the friendship. Then came the bite: While he was busy with the host's wife, what were the host and his own wife doing?

Then there was the girl who tabbed herself as a swinger but still a virgin at 22 who wanted to remain so until marriage; however, all her dates dropped her when they discovered she wasn't going to put out. What to do, did all men, and so forth. She was told that many men would respect her wishes if they knew what they were but if she acted, talked and dressed like a swinger but didn't want to play swinging games, she should tell her dates at once. After all, the Advisor said, if you look, walk and quack like a duck, you can't blame men for thinking you are a duck.

Such social quandaries as these are sprinkled with requests for factual information about stereo systems and how various things originated—like applause, or the term fourth estate. Matters of etiquette come up, and pleas to settle bets, fashion questions—all the things, big and small, that interest people.

This department or feature of Playboy is not, of course, an unusual one for any publication—most have them in some form—but it's so well and tastefully handled that it's no wonder it has such a high readership rating. If it doesn't rate as a circulation puller, it does as a circulation pleaser.

And that *Playboy* has plenty of those is evidenced by its most recent spectacular gain in circulation—one million more in 1971 than in 1970, or a record high of 6,700,000. This will enable it to increase its circulation rate base from 5,250,000 to six million this July.

The most striking thing about that circulation rise is that most of it—791,817—came in the last six months of 1971. The June 30 closing figure was quoted as 5,908,183 in a table rating 25 of the leading U.S. magazines. *Playboy* was in eleventh place with *Look* in tenth. With *Look* defunct, *Playboy* automatically rose to tenth and with its new 6,700,000 is right on the heels of *Ladies Home Journal* with 7,056,468.

194

The other eight ahead are *National Geographic*, with 7,210, 143; *Life*, 7,228,299; *Family Circle*, 7,474, 101; *McCall's*, 7,515,235; *Woman's Day*, 7,517,151; *Better Homes and Gardens*, 7,908,718; *TV Guide*, 16,211,999, and *Reader's Digest*, 18,159,787.

Another odd note about *Playboy's* circulation—in percentages it has hovered around 76 percent single copy sales and 24 percent subscriptions since 1962. This is the reverse of most magazines' circulation pattern. But management believes it is more profitable and continues to plug newsstand sales even while going after subscriptions through direct mail advertising, cards inserted in issues, sales reps on college campuses, pre-distribution publicity releases and newsstand displays.

Playboy's original newsstand price of 50 cents per copy did not change until September 1960, when it went to 60 cents; it was upped to 75 cents in September 1963 and then in February 1969 went to $1. The price for each December and January issue has been 40 or 50 cents higher than the other ten issues since December 1961. It now seems steady at 50.

As *Playboy's* price has increased, so has its number of editorial pages. A 300-page issue is common. Its proportion of editorial pages to advertising pages is considered to be one of the highest in publishing. *Playboy's* ratio of 65-70 percent editorial to 35-30 percent advertising compares with 55 percent editorial to 45 percent advertising in the average consumer magazine.

In the beginning, there was no particular incentive to subscribe to the magazine, because the one-year subscription price was $6, the same total as the newsstand price per year. It remained $6 when the single copy price went to 60 cents. Then, in 1963 it began to edge upward when the price became $7 in September. It went to $8 in July 1964 and in February 1969 to $10, or $3 below the newsstand price annually.

So Hefner has compromised, if only slightly, with his first policy in publishing *Playboy*—a policy of no reduced rates for subscription sales. But that seems to have come about naturally as the circulation grew. He has not compromised the policy by any of the gimmicks other magazines use—such as offering introductory subscriptions at lower than the going rate.

The magazine is distributed through two outlets: For subscription mailing, labels are produced from nameplates and sent to an outside firm that wraps each copy in a plain brown wrapper, sticks on the label and handles the mailing.

For newsstand sales, the Independent News Company distributes 80 percent of each press run to magazine wholesalers. They sell to individual retailers. All copies are sold on consignment. Independent pays 58 percent of the retail price; the wholesaler 64 percent, and the retailer 80 percent.

Except for the Playmate of the Month centerfold, W.F. Hall Printing Co. of Chicago prints and binds *Playboy* magazine under a contract that will run through the May issue of 1981. Hall has been printing the magazine since 1955. About three-fourths of the paper used is supplied by Kimberly-Clark Corp. and its contract expires on December 31, 1975. The contract obligates *Playboy* to purchase paper in the minimum annual amount of nine million dollars but needs have always exceeded the minimum. With Hall, prices are subject to adjustments for changes in the costs of labor, material and other contingencies.

Hefner has had a running battle with censors who have started proceedings contending that *Playboy*, or a particular issue, is obscene. None of those filed in the U.S. has resulted in such a ruling. (Hefner was once arrested after the magazine published nude photographs of Jayne Mansfield, but that case ended in a hung jury.) However, *Playboy* is banned in some foreign countries and in others, some issues have been prohibited.

Internationally, the U.S. issue of the magazine is distributed by a February 1966 acquisition costing $579,000, Boarts International Inc., in Puerto Rico and Canada. Fairly recently, a United Kingdom and a German edition have been born and Playboy is eyeing several other locations abroad.

And here's a good spot to dispose of a legend, the kind that inevitably had to grow up around Hefner. I was often asked what the little stars inside the "P" of the *Playboy* name on the cover mean. The silly—if not insane—legend is that they represent how Hefner rates the sexability of the girl on the front cover, how good she is in bed. The prosaic truth is that it's a fancy way of designating—for advertising purposes—which region a particular copy is bound for; that is, international, Midwest, East or West Coast, and so on. The reason this key is necessary is because, while editorial matter remains the same, different advertising is inserted in the different regional issues; also, for shipping purposes.

Hefner's second policy in publishing *Playboy* concerns the sale of advertising space. An acceptance committee screens all prospective ads to make sure that they complement the concept of the magazine. Ads are not accepted if they don't, or if they are in poor taste, are too flamboyant, push too hard, are not attractively presented or are uncomplimentary to the young male reader's ego.

Playboy will not carry ads for such ego-affronting products as hair restorers, toupees and reducing aids. It also will not run ads aimed at women despite the fact that more than four million females read *Playboy* each month. And ads for nude films and marriage manuals that other men's magazines often carry are also taboo in *Playboy*. Instead, ad pages are filled with men's apparel advertising (more than $5 million a year worth), alcoholic beverages (about $6 million worth), and men's toiletries and smoking products. *Playboy* also carries auto advertising from Ford, Chrysler and American Motors, along with many foreign car manufacturers. Conspicuously missing among the auto makers is General Motors, which refuses to advertise in the magazine because it doesn't like *Playboy's* image.

Howard Lederer directs a staff of 30 full-time salesmen working out of offices in New York, Chicago, Detroit, Atlanta, Los Angeles and London. *Playboy* reaches more than seven million men in the 18-to-34-year-old group and the median age of a *Playboy* reader is about 29 years old. This makes the *Playboy* readership an attractive group to an advertiser.

Advertising page rates are set by the company and are based on a specified level of average net paid circulation. As circulation has increased, so has the circulation base and the advertising page rate. With the July establishment of a new base rate, the cost for a four-color ad page, for instance, will rise from $36,542 to $42,950, resulting in a cost-per-thousand reduction from $7.42 to $7.16.

As a consequence of *Playboy's* huge circulation explosion in 1971, advertising revenue topped $35 million, an 11 percent gain over 1970, and the number of ad pages carried went went from 904 in 1970 to 948, or 9 percent more.

In a "Memo to Advertisers" inserted between the inside front cover and Page 1 of the January 1972 issue *Playboy* trumpeted, "Another Year of Bountiful Bonuses" and gave a month-by-month rundown of the number of bonus copies delivered over the rate base of 4,800,000 it started with in January. (The base was changed to 5,250,000 in October.)

The point being made was that advertisers had received a bonus because exposure of their ads was, as in January, in 1,252,000 copies more than they had paid for on the rate base; in February, 1,177,000; March, 1,004,000; April, 1,001,000; May, 1,029,000; June, 1,186,000, and similar figures through the year.

Strong competitors for the kind of ad revenues *Playboy* seeks are *Esquire, Gentleman's Quarterly* and *Sports Illustrated.*

Playboy magazine has always had its imitators—*Escapade, Cavalier, Modern Man, Caper* and *Dude*—none of which worried it because none came anywhere close to being a threat in the subscription or advertising departments.

The strongest challenger yet is Bob Guccione's *Penthouse*, which first hit the stands in England in 1964. It's not as sophisticated as *Playboy* and was at one time much bolder. *Playboy*, scenting an interloper, has moved to counteract that with more open photography.

However, that Guccione, 41, has declared war on *Playboy*

and Hefner is no trade secret. He has plainly said that he's out to be the top totem on the men's magazine pole and he's kicked up quite a fuss here and there trying to accomplish that feat.

Guccione's background is totally beyond the life experience of Hefner. As a youth he was constantly being arrested for vagrancy in California and driven to the state line, where he promptly thumbed his way back to Los Angeles.

Somehow he got to Europe and at one time or another was an artist, an actor, a fortune teller and a dry cleaner. The latter job turned him into a businessman when he introduced 24-hour cleaning to England and within a short time was running the company.

Guccione's period as a recluse was much shorter and for an entirely different reason than Hefner's. His was for a two-week period while he edited the first issue of *Penthouse* and it was in order to avoid arrest in London. He had attracted unfavorable attention from postal authorities by having printed on credit 800,000 sales brochures for the magazine and sending them to a mail-order list of prospects. Though the response was financially a bonanza, the postal department objected to the brochures because they featured eight nudes.

The day the first *Penthouse* issue went on sale, Guccione's trial was front-paged, surely no coincidence, and he paid a fine of $308 for sending indecent literature through the mail. But that was a small price to pay to reap about $80,000 that the sell-out of the 120,000 copies brought him.

Guccione now claims his magazine sells 200,000 in Britain to *Playboy's* 90,000 and also outsells it in France and Vietnam, in addition to 500,000 in the U.S.

Playboy has decided to go continental this year, setting up separate editions in Italy, France and Germany. Competition will be tough because of the plethora of girlie magazines already on European newsstands. Observers say that Hefner was encouraged to go into Europe by the fact that *Penthouse* is doing well there. (Rosenzweig once told *Executive Magazine*: "One thing Hefner demands in every venture he goes into is control, which is why the magazine [*Playboy*] will never be published in a foreign language.") *Playboy* will be printed in the respective language of each country. About 70 percent of the magazine's content will be drawn from the U.S. edition, with the balance contributed by the writers of each country. And as for the centerfolds of the European *Playboys*, they will be graced by the young ladies of Europe.

Hefner's rival is also squaring off to compete with him on the club level—he has a club-casino in London and plans for others in such places as Milan, Rome and New York.

But if Guccione blasted off in the beginning, he's created quite some to-do in the U.S. in advertising and TV circles and has underlined his huff-and-puff tactics against Hefner with ads and commercials depicting the Playboy Rabbit dripping one distinct tear over Penthouse circulation gains. ABC-TV at first accepted the commercial and it was supposed to start running in January of this year—but upon second thought, ABC rejected it, giving as a reason that it was "disparaging" to a competitor. CBS and NBC also turned it down and it finally was placed on Metromedia's chain. The ads appearing in newspapers carry a line that the rabbit is the registered trademark of HMH Publishing Co., Inc., adding that "there is no connection between Penthouse International Ltd. and HMH."

The former Catholic altar boy has picked himself a formidable champ to put on the gloves with. Maybe that population explosion will be big enough so that there's room for twins on top of the totem pole.

Another *Playboy*-styled magazine was introduced last February. Called *Gallery*, the monthly had an initial run of 200,000 copies and a newsstand price of a dollar. *Gallery's* publisher is the well-known criminal lawyer, F. Lee Bailey. Gallery Enterprises Corporation has plans for a $2.5-million stock offering in the near future. And what's a Playboy-type magazine without a Playboy-type club? Gallery also anticipates opening a Gallery Club in Chicago.

Playboy, as can be seen, is fat and growing fatter.

Another aspect of the phenomenon is that millions of

women read *Playboy*. It seems odd, at first, but after awhile it's not so odd. Playboy claims the inside track to the thoughts and desires of the young sophisticate, so what better way for his women to find out about his innermost preferences and yearnings? That has to be the way they think—they'd hardly read it for the love of bare bosoms and bottoms.

Anyway, after all my research, and finding out more about *Playboy* than anybody needs to know, I came to the unoriginal conclusion that what spells *Playboy*, fundamentally, is those same shapely bare bosoms and bottoms treated with such tender, loving care in presentation, production and circulation and advertising know-how.

An "insider's" publication, the little sister of *Playboy* magazine that goes only to keyholders, is called *VIP* and it's been the Little Orphan Annie at Playboy Enterprises for years. The editorial staff looks down on it as a promotion project and the promotion staff looks at it as an editorial project. The result was a weak, meaningless production.

But in April or May of 1970, Hefner and I met in the Mansion for approximately twelve hours and discussed the revamping of *VIP*. Spectorsky and Murray Fisher, one of his senior editors, had assumed the titles of editor and contributing editor, respectively. In reality, however, they served no function other than to periodically issue a long, obtuse memo or two saying how bad *VIP* was. It lacked any real direction, any real purpose. Nobody ever asked what it was supposed to accomplish, what it was trying to do, what purpose it should serve.

If they had done so, they would have realized that *VIP* should have been almost totally a vehicle by which Playboy Club members were apprised of the more positive aspects of the clubs and hotels. It also could be used as a sales promotion organ to stimulate the continued interest of keyholders in the clubs and hotels.

Because nobody decided this, everyone simply assumed it was some vague editorial output, the purpose of which was to publicize Playboy clubs or hotels and related activities, or else it was a magazine that appealed to the Playboy Club type of audience, which is older than *Playboy* itself. They tried to accomplish these questionable objectives by simply taking *Playboy's* reject material and stuffing that into *VIP* as filler. That is the editorial flavor it took and it was a pretty foul flavor.

A frequent basis for editorial judgment as to whether or not something should appear in *VIP* was if plates had been made for a *Playboy* article and the article was pulled at the last minute, wasting the cost of the plates. Now that is one helluva way to protect the investment of many millions of dollars in clubs and hotels, but nobody thought of that.

I remember one of the most ridiculous articles ever to appear was a *Playboy* reject after plates were made. It was called "The Bunny is Fine Art." It took the Mona Lisa and put rabbit ears on her, it took the Venus de Milo and put a bunny tail on her and so on, and this was to be a full-color, three-page spread.

Anyway, Hefner and I worked out the specific purpose that *VIP* ought to serve and it was decided that I would assume its editorial direction as one of my various functions, even though I'd had no editorial experience. Hefner felt that I could handle it better if for no other reason than that nobody else seemed to understand what the motivations behind *VIP* ought to be.

I became the editor of *VIP* and from then on part of my time was spent judging everything from the editorial content and the art direction to determining the advisability, for example, of sending six models, photographers, an art director and two editorial writers to Miami Beach to cover the Playboy Plaza opening.

It really was a simple task, it merely required the understanding of a direction and some attempt to achieve it.

Chapter 16
Press, Playmates and Photography

It was a running fight at Playboy over executives giving information to the press. The public relations department was supposed to clear all statements but many executives attempted to bypass PR in order to publicize themselves.

That happened when we were buying the Playboy Plaza in Florida. A PCI executive was negotiating the details of the contract and broke the story on his own, disregarding our plans completely.

An elaborate press kit had been prepared by the public relations department and it was to be presented at a press luncheon the day after the signing of the contract.

Despite this, the PCI executive called a Miami reporter the night before the signing and spilled all the details of it. The following day, when the story was published, much of it was unfavorable because he had shot his load too quickly and with some erroneous and negative information that could have been avoided. That episode typifies the kind of thing that occurred constantly.

That executive was reprimanded by Morton and Preuss,

who walked around saying things like "get rid of him, he's no damned good." But he was one of Morton's pets, and wasn't fired.

So, although no one is supposed to give information directly to the press, when they can slide it by PR they do. I did it on several occasions but only because the final responsibility for dissemination of information to the press was mine.

The press is receptive to any information about what goes on at Playboy so it's easy to move a story. Any number of people will pick it up. In Chicago, of course, Maggie Daly, Irv Kupcinet, Joe Cappo, the Andersons (Jon and Abra) and George Lazarus. All of them would usually use an item on a minute's notice. On a national basis, never any TV news coverage because that is not Playboy's medium, but in national gossip columns, such as Earl Wilson's, it was the easiest thing in the world to get something in there. And even if TV isn't Playboy's medium, to get something mentioned on talk shows was no problem at all. A favorite Playboy PR ploy is to invite columnists from around the country to spend a few days at the Mansion.

Playboy tries to suppress unfavorable items, naturally. One of them was the disappearance of a former general manager of two Playboy clubs. Another was the huge fluff about the Bunny at the New York club who wrote the district attorney and the state liquor commission, telling about being beaten by the hoods hanging out at the club and how the general manager and his assistant wanted her and the other Bunnies to put out for the hoods.

Then there were a couple of articles directly related to Hefner that we tried to suppress. One was the long memo that Hefner wrote about women's lib and how to treat it in the magazine. That got out, though, and appeared in *Seed*. And there were the invasion of the Playboy Mansion by women's lib groups and the defacing of the walls of the Mansion by militant women's liberationists.

Another incident that got limited exposure involved a Bunny who was accosted behind the Playboy Mansion at 2 a.m. one morning. What was she doing behind the Mansion at that hour in the first place? Her explanation was simple enough: "I was looking for my contact lens." (No wonder she didn't see her attacker.)

Things got out accidentally or on purpose or just through plain stupidity. Occasionally, an executive was warned to keep his mouth shut, either to the press or in speeches.

One top executive, for instance, was told never again to give speeches that conveyed negativism about Playboy. Preuss reprimanded him about a slide presentation he made to a large group that contained a lot of negative talk about the company and sly innuendoes about Hefner.

And there was another marketing director who was subsequently fired. He had to be told to keep off liquor in public places. He was a heavy drinker and the first day he was with Playboy, he and Preuss and Morton went to dinner at the VIP Room at the Playboy Club. He got up during dinner and began asking the patrons what they thought of the club. He was doing his own little on-the-spot research but he was three-quarters sauced. Preuss told him to confine his dining to dining and not to interviewing—and to keep off the booze in public.

The business press has been generally favorable toward Playboy over the years. Hefner and Playboy have been written about by every major business publication in the country except for perhaps the most prestigious one—*Fortune*. And this snub has bothered those Playboy executives who are especially hungry for recognition as businessmen.

Hefner was often greatly displeased by what appeared about him in some articles. One that threw him into a rage, mouthing obscenities, was a story in *New York* magazine about his trip to Acapulco with Bernie Cornfeld.

In the winter of 1970 Hefner and Cornfeld met for several days in a villa called "Nirvana" in Acapulco to plan big things for that part of Mexico. The plan called for the development of a $15-million, 32-story, 512-unit condominium. Cornfeld was to provide the capital and Playboy was to run the condominium as semi-hotels with Playboy Clubs.

Hefner left the security of the Mansion in Chicago with all his security symbols—pipe, Pepsi-Colas and Barbi—arriving in good shape aboard the sleek, ebonized Big Bunny bearing the white rabbit on its tail. Cornfeld left his 12th Century castle in France with his bag of tricks, too—mink coat, lumberjack hat and Jackie—coming out of the sky in his sleek white Falcon with the red Swiss cross on its tail. Bernie's entourage also included a secretary, two lawyers, and to Hefner's dismay, astute journalist Julie Baumgold, who described the two playboys as "Big Daddies with their false kids."

Ms. Baumgold followed the pair with an eagle eye and keen ear, tracking them to the perimeter of their private and public lives—their bedroom doors. (From that point, imagination must take over.)

The deal never did materialize, partly, I suppose, because of Cornfeld's financial troubles. But maybe it was doomed from the start for the two titans of hedonism who met in "Nirvana" to plan big things. By Webster's definition, "Nirvana" is in Buddhism "the state of perfect blessedness achieved by the extinction of individual existence and by absorption of the soul into the supreme spirit, or by the extinction of all desires and passions." According to that definition, neither Hefner nor Cornfeld really had any business in "Nirvana."

Gutwillig, Preuss and I were conferring with Hefner when Gutwillig produced a proof of Julie's article that had been supplied to him by a friend at the magazine just before it hit the newsstands. Hefner read it and was absolutely livid, talking about "that bitch Baumgold" and how Cornfeld was so stupid as to have invited a spy on the trip. Hefner's words for Cornfeld were just plain nasty. Julie Baumgold quoted Cornfeld as implying that Hefner really wasn't such a neat fellow and his women were pretty mediocre and he only had one plane and so on.

Hefner stormed up and down the conference room, sucking frantically on his pipe, saying "that idiot Cornfeld, if he wants to do business with us, why is he talking about me like that?"

A day or two later I was in Hefner's office when Cornfeld called from Switzerland and Hefner asked him why he had said those things. After hearing what Cornfeld had to say about it, Hefner said, "All right, Bernie, I understand." When he hung up he didn't reveal Cornfeld's explanation.

I guess Playboy's best PR vehicle is still the Playmate.

A very closely held privilege at Playboy was attendance at the Playmate photographic shootings.

The motivation was nothing as valid as thoughtfulness for the girl—that a crowd on the set would embarrass her. Admission to the shootings was a favor doled out by Tajiri to close friends and associates. And then only if he owed them a favor or wanted to put them in debt to him.

As a result, some of the Playmate shootings took on aspects of a pornographic film shooting at 42nd Street in New York, where the attendance fee includes cameras—with no film in them.

The Playboy photographers took their relationships with the Playmates in a very serious way, so they were offended by Tajiri's tactics. On his part, Tajiri looked on it with the sensitivity of a pimp and his only concern was how many favors would be owed to him at the end of each shooting.

I had not done any favors for Tajiri but after I became marketing director I needed to attend Playmate shootings to direct the photography incorporating the use of the Playmates for promotional purposes.

In previous years, there had always been a 10-minute section of the photographic session devoted to promotion. For example, for Christmas subscription ads, invariably the Playmate was posed holding a sprig of mistletoe or a holly wreath in front of her crotch and that was considered suitable.

I objected to this stupid stereotype and decided I would have to attend one or more of the shootings.

"Vince," I said, when I got him on the phone, "I'd like to come to your next two or three Playmate shootings and see if we can work out something besides mistletoe and holly wreath crotch shots for the Christmas ads."

207

"Absolutely not," he said, without a moment's hesitation, "those shootings are closed and you know it."

"They shouldn't be closed to me," I answered, "this is business, I'm not interested in gaping at naked girls."

"No," he said again, "it would upset the girls. I won't admit you to the set. If you want to, you can tell the photographer roughly what you want and if he agrees, we'll try to shoot it that way."

"Vince," I said, as patiently as I could, "that's ridiculous. If I can't see the girl being photographed, and have a chance to judge her camera personality, it'd be impossible to decide the best way to pose her for what I want. You know that's true, Vince."

It was true and he did know it but he was just too obstinate to admit it. He kept saying no, so I finally took it to Hefner and Hefner, through a memo written by Rosenzweig, advised Tajiri that I was to be allowed on the set and that my requests were to be met.

When I arrived on the set for the shooting of Claudia Jennings, who was the Playmate of the Year in 1970, I found the company consulting architect; the PCI accounting manager; the promotion art director, who worked for me; the photographer shooting the spread, Dwight Hooker; two standby photographers; one of the promotion associate art directors; an associate picture editor, Marilyn Grabowski; one camera grip; Vince; Dee Dante, the gal who served as liaison between the Playmate and the company, and a fellow named Tom Owens, who was the home living editor, or the products editor.

So much for Tajiri's insistence that I would disrupt the set or disturb the Playmate—the truth is, no one noticed me in the crowd.

By the issue of April 1972 there had been two hundred and twenty-two Playmates and only two had gotten into trouble seriously enough to make the headlines—one charged with prostitution, a charge that was later withdrawn, and one with smuggling thirty-eight pounds of hashish into Greece from Turkey, for which she was convicted and sentenced to ten months in jail. This was one month after she appeared in the centerfold and at the memory of it Futch turns pale and shudders.

None of them has gone as far as the first—Marilyn Monroe—but several have been grabbed for movies or TV or married men moderately famous in their own right. Most have dropped from sight after their brief fling at glory.

After hitting the jackpot with the Monroe blast in the first issue, Hefner set the pattern of what the centerfold girl should be that has been followed all the months and years since: he found an average, but well-endowed, girl in the subscription department, Charlene Drain, and persuaded her to pose by promising to provide her department with an Addressograph machine she said was needed. She became "Janet Pilgrim" for photo purposes and was, until she married and went to Texas, head of the readers' service department. She was the inspiration for *Playboy's* "girl next door" Playmate concept. Janet Pilgrim holds the distinction of being the only Playmate featured in the centerfold three different times—July 1955, December 1955 and October 1956. The name survived and is still on the masthead.

But only two blots out of two hundred and twenty-two young and relatively inexperienced, unworldly girls is fantastic and the reason for it is the strictures that govern selection of Playmates.

The Playmate candidates are located in a variety of ways. A photographic studio in California has found a great many. Free-lance photographers find them on beaches or at weddings or parties or on college campuses, in some guy's office, even walking down the street. A lot of girls write in, large numbers of photographs are sent in—most of these are sent back as unsuitable.

But some have tried to keep from getting into the magazine at the last minute and have been unable to do so because they had signed a release. In virtually every such case, they use as a reason the fact that they have falsified some of the statements in the release, age or name or something like that.

(One girl did achieve the impossible, but she had to take to prayer—and Hugh Hefner—to do it. According to an Associated Press dispatch in February, Debbie Hanlon, 19, of Royal Oak, Michigan, who is studying to become a member of Jehovah's Witnesses, decided it would be immoral. The contract had been signed, the picture of her lying nude on a green-and-white polka-dotted sheet had been taken and the layout was set for the April 1972 issue. But Debbie "prayed like mad" and talked Hefner into dropping it.)

That's why *Playboy* checks out all information prior to committing itself to the publication of the photograph. To my knowledge, there's never been an instance of a press run being held up, although *Playboy* has been sued several times by Playmates for running their photographs after they decided they didn't want them published. None of them were successful. It's pretty hard for an 18-year-old girl to get good enough counsel to defeat the Playboy Enterprises lineup of attorneys.

Eighteen to twenty-one are the age limits for the girls. They must have a virginal quality that the camera can catch— the All-American, girl-next-door look, wholesome and fresh, like a college football team cheerleader. They must never have posed for or had published a nude picture, never have held a job as a topless go-go girl or stripper. Bunnies, who bare almost as much, are the sole exceptions to this rule and many have become Playmates.

Other criteria include having a goodlooking enough body and face to photograph well; being willing to pose in the nude and to sign a release to that effect; doing it for $5,000, which is not the greatest amount in the world; enough intelligence so they can be used for *Playboy* promotions; they must not be alcoholics or junkies who would foul up some public relations effort; and they must have led a clean enough life, at least on the surface, so that *Playboy* is not embarrassed by publicity that one of their Playmates is a stripper named Gorgeous Gertie.

The trademark of the Playmate, of course, is the Rubenesque figure—Hefner insists on pneumatic breasts, although occasionally one slips by who doesn't have outsize ornaments. But on no account can breasts sag. Ideally, the girl must be caught just as her growth is complete, before there is even the slightest droop. This is the reason for the age limitation and why single girls are preferred to married, particularly mothers. Childbirth generally ruins a girl's figure for *Playboy's* purposes.

Nevertheless, although *Playboy* tries to conceal it, about one-third of the girls are married. *Playboy* has to use married women sometimes because there aren't enough eligible single women around who can fulfill all the requirements.

Photographers are always on the lookout for Playmate candidates for one reason only—the loot, which is $6,000 for three weeks to a month's work. When one of the camera clan finds a likely prospect, he ships about one hundred nude shots of her to Chicago, where they come under the eye, first, of Marilyn Grabowski. Marilyn gets about fifty of these batches a month and when she finds a "possible" she mails out the fifty-question *Playboy* Data Sheet and the mechanics of selecting a Playmate are underway.

When the data sheet is returned, Marilyn routes it and a selection of the pictures to about a dozen editors and art and photo directors—like Kessie, Paul and Tajiri. Each votes privately to accept, reject, or hold for more tests. Rejection usually is on the basis of too small breasts, too skinny thighs or because the girl looks like a tramp.

Only if the majority vote to accept does Hefner get his first look at the hopefuls and out of a dozen he may accept two. Hefner tries to balance out the number of blondes, brunettes and redheads and will latch onto an occasional Eurasian or black beauty to provide variety.

The next step is the authorized photographing for the centerfold layout. Staff photographers do about 60 percent of these and their first two decisions are whether the girl will look better in a horizontal or a vertical position, and whether she will be more photogenic in an indoor or an outdoor setting. Of course, the month the picture is to be published comes heavily into that decision. Summer is usually outdoors, winter indoors.

No body makeup is used but a makeup man is paid $100 a day (Jerry Whitezel, when I was there) to keep the girls looking the way they're supposed to—and that is natural. Sometimes he has to remove several layers of this and that to get down to the girl and start over to achieve that natural look.

The photographer must keep several things in mind—good taste is the credo, there must be no hint of pornography. And, oddly enough, he must see that the studio temperature is just right—too cool and the girl gets goosebumps; too warm and she sags.

The shooting continues until Hefner is satisfied that the best possible picture has been taken for the centerfold. Then the supporting shots are made, and this may entail travel anywhere in the world.

The filming sessions usually last from four to five hours and the photographer may take as many as four hundred pictures. It's an expensive proposition—the eight-by-ten Deardorff is always used and the film costs $2.30 per exposure. It costs another $2.70 for developing it into a color transparency, so four hundred exposures add up to $2,000. The supporting candids, about 3,000 in 35mm., cost another $2,000. Then there's $5,000 to the Playmate and a number of other expenses. Add them all up and it costs *Playboy* around $20,000 a month per Playmate spread. But when Hefner wants perfection, he's willing to pay for it, and perfection is the only thing he will accept for the Playmates.

Hefner is an expert at judging nude photography, proving that practice makes perfect. He, of course, is an expert at judging any photography. He and I went over batches of transparencies, anything from the party at the London club, his trip to Africa, the houseboat in Florida, advertising promotion photos, to the nudes. And, although my judgments were pretty good, anyway, prior to my sessions with him, I benefited from them.

I remember particularly that once we had a table top strewn with about fifty transparencies of the same girl and we were trying to make a decision as to which was the best.

"She looks very, very natural here," I said, picking one up and showing it to Hefner. "She has a charming little smile on her face and her body looks natural, looks at ease, she doesn't look forced."

"Yes," he agreed, scanning it, "but you see how the dark shadow is getting in there on the side of her face?"

"We could lighten that up," I agreed, "but come to think of it, we can't put a glisten in her eyes like she has in the other transparencies."

"True," he said, flipping rapidly through some of the others. "Here's a good one but look, one breast is shorter than the other one."

"We can retouch that, but we can't fill out her hip," I noted. Either it really was on the scrawny side or the angle from which it had been taken made it look so. You can take away with retouching but you can't add on.

And so it went. On this particular occasion Hefner and I, independently, picked the same one as the choicest of the lot. But then, our judgments were frequently identical.

Judging of photographs comprises both tangibles and intangibles, technicalities and aesthetics. It is a matter of recognizing sales appeal, in the same way you decide what kind of merchandise is going to sell. There are intangible ingredients you look for to determine whether or not something is the most salable, the most promotable, or the most comprehensive to the viewer. You're looking for things that you feel about a photograph as well as things that you specifically point to and say, "This is too light or this is too dark."

But the biggest thing in deciding about the centerfold nudes is the expression on a girl's face and how that is going to be responded to. Is someone going to look at it and say, "Huh, she looks like a slut," or "Huh, she really has a certain Madonna look to her."

You may examine one transparency and the girl will look trampy, she'll have a slatternly look in her eyes. I don't know exactly how you discern a slatternly look, but you just know when you look at it. Then tangible things come up, not only of lighting but of composition. If the natural pose of the girl, the natural angle of the photograph, cause the girl's crotch to be covered, that's fine. But if she's just standing there with her hand over it, that looks foolish.

The things that Hefner told me in going over hundreds and hundreds of transparencies helped me to refine and strengthen my own opinions. We reaffirmed each other because our tastes were so similar—except in active photographing.

My camera equipment can be inspected daily from 9 to 5, but he never monkeys around with cameras at all. Perhaps that is because it would get him too involved; it would bring him too close to the subject matter and cause him to relate too much to what he is photographing.

(We also had similar tastes about art. Hefner views a painting as something decorative, pleasing to look at, but which you generally do not get a really strong feeling toward. A piece of sculpture, however, was different. It was a more moving art form, evoking a more intense aesthetic feeling than did a painting.)

The Playmates, of course, get plenty of exposure while they are Playmates, plenty of publicity through promotions they are put into, the more intelligent of them. But the general intelligence level is not high, as witness the book, *The Girl in the Centerfold*, "written" by a former Playmate. Having bared everything else, she apparently felt the urge to bare her soul and it must be one of the worst books ever published. It bombed, of course, because it was so vulgar, so cheap; it made such an effort to be sensational that it turned the reader off, or anybody else who was so unfortunate as to pick it up, God forbid pay good money for it.

The side of the coin the ex-Playmate-author never turns is the one Dee Dante was happy to reveal: "Many . . . don't believe in drugs, sleeping around or drinking. Some are married and are helping put their husbands through school, were virgins when they married and have no intention of going to bed with someone else."

I don't agree with Dee that "many" of the girls weren't drinkers or drug takers or didn't sleep around. But the twenty-five or so I knew either drank, took dope or fucked like rabbits. (One Bunny, I recall, proudly boasted about the baby she had aborted whose father is one of the celebrities who often stays at the Mansion.) Dee is entitled to her opinion, of course—as promotion coordinator and beauty counselor she was closer to the girls than their mothers, so maybe she knew more than I did.

Dee "escaped" Playboy when she was reconverted to Catholicism, which had been her childhood religion and from which she had strayed in college. She had been divorced but she was accepted as a Third Order member of the Carmelite nuns. That is, she is now a lay sister who takes the same vows as all Carmelites—obedience, poverty and chastity—but who works and lives outside the convent.

I hear that Dee, too, is writing a book—about the things she taught the Playmates and their beauty secrets. Dee is a lovely, sweet person who believes in good grooming as well as God and I'm sure that her book cannot be the trashy muck that that ex-Playmate turned out.

To get back to the mechanics of producing the Playmate of the Month centerfold layout, before the candids are shot a story line is decided upon, depending upon the girl's interests or hobbies. If she's a complete blank, they settle for "a day in the life of." Half the shots are color nudes and half black and white story line.

These go to Tajiri. He and an assistant pick about 200 and they are sent to the art department for layout. It's five pages and usually pretty much the same from month to month, although there is some room for creativeness.

It is only after Hefner has approved a layout that the writer gets his innings and this task is rotated among the writers to keep it fresh in presentation. The text then must be approved by Kessie and Hefner and at last the copy is set, positioned in the layout and the job is ready to go to the printer.

While W.H. Hall prints the rest of *Playboy*, the centerfold goes to Regensteiner Printing. Both are Chicago-based. Regensteiner is considered a top four-color lithographic outfit and the man who oversees the reproduction of the centerfold is Art Johnson, who's been in the business since 1929. An etcher named Julius Block makes the engravings and proofs are sent to Hefner. Sometimes the etching has to be redone because it doesn't please Hefner and he'll order changes. When the etching is finally approved, preliminary proofs are run off and go to Hefner for final approval.

But that's not the end of it—samples of the first sheets off the press also go to Hefner and frequently he will order the presses stopped and more red (which he equates with warmth) used.

It all costs—but Playboys must have perfect Playmates.

Chapter 17
The Cost of A Social Conscience

On the social consciousness scoreboard, at least some of the people at Playboy have to rate as public liberals and private bigots. And in some cases, just plain hypocrites.

The incident of the two black attorneys is typical. They were the only black professionals out of 4,000 Playboy employees.

Preuss called me in the summer of 1970 and said, "We have two black attorneys and neither of them does much for us but I'm afraid that if we get rid of both of them at once the American Civil Liberties Union or some other faction is going to be on our backs. We have to handle it judiciously and get rid of one of them now and the other maybe six or eight months from now." Preuss gave his reasons and I agreed with him. However, I said, "I think we ought to fire both of them."

"But we can't fire both of them" he said.

"If these two guys were white you would fire both of them," I said.

"Yes," he returned, "but they're not white."

"Dammit, Bob," I said, "that's hypocritical. Those guys ought to be fired because they're not doing the job for the company and that should be the only reason that's given to anyone because it is the only reason. We couldn't care less if they were purple." But Preuss wouldn't agree, so we fired only one.

An example of covert bigotry involved a Playboy executive and *Essence*, the black woman's magazine. He was ostensibly an ultra-liberalist who had previously worked for a major publishing company.

The first knowledge I had that this man was not what he cracked himself up to be was when he called me one day from New York. I had him on the squawk box, the speaker phone, which I used sometimes if other people needed to hear the conversation or if I wanted to keep my hands free to take notes.

He didn't know it, but then in my office was a young fellow who had resigned from the research department several weeks earlier and who was telling me some of his views on Playboy. I asked the executive when he would be back from New York and he said, "Oh, as soon as I get finished with the spades."

"What do you mean?" I asked.

"I'm with the niggers," he said, "I'm with these people at *Essence*, the coons, dig?"

"If someone were overhearing this," I said, and I was about to tell him someone was, "your jocular comments could sound bigoted."

"Jocular my ass," he said, in a very serious tone, and added, "Listen, what I called you about . . . "

The social involvement of a corporation may be somewhat more extensive than the involvement of the individuals comprising the corporation because it is easier to give money as a group or as a corporation than it is to become personally involved.

For instance, Playboy money helped finance the political campaign of a popular Illinois congressman. In a conversation with Preuss and Hefner the reason came out: The congressman guaranteed that if Playboy contributed sizably to his campaign, he would urge the defeat of any bill having to do with pornography sent through the mails, or postal reform acts of any sort that would be detrimental to *Playboy*. This was a clearcut consideration in return for $25,000 for a congressman's campaign fund, as stated by Preuss to Hefner and myself. Now, $25,000 is not a small chunk for a representative. It's a pretty hefty contribution.

But on the corporation's involvement, the HMH Publishing Co. Inc.'s promotion expense analysis for the year ended June 30, 1970, contains the total of Playboy Foundation grants for that year. Contributions were $62,096.64. Listed, with the largest first, were:

. Sex Information and Education Council of the U.S., $10,000. An interview with the head of SIECUS, Mary Calderone, was done. And with it came the right to use that interview in promotional materials to secure advertising and circulation.

Clergy Consultation Service, for problem pregnancies, $10,000.

Rabinowitz bond and standard legal expenses regarding Timothy Leary (the LSD and drug advocate), $6,428. Playboy was granted certain promotional rights to the *Playboy* interview with Leary, which had been conducted earlier.

National Association for the Advancement of Colored People, legal fund, $5,000. I assume this was an out-an-out donation, as was perhaps another $5,000 to Lowe Center for Constitutional Rights.

National Broadcasting Co., television promotion, $5,000.

Committee for Effective Drug Abuse Legislation, $2,500. The magazine did an article on the use of drugs.

Black Legislative Clearing House, $2,500.

Association for Family Living, $1,500—to help pay for an ad in the *Chicago Tribune* regarding sex education.

Also, sixteen tickets costing $1,200 were purchased for a dinner honoring Coretta Scott King, wife of the late Dr. Martin Luther King, Jr. The rest of the donations were for totals of $1,500 or $1,000.

So, of the total of $62,096, at least $25,000 is of questionable nature as to whether or not it did not give Playboy at least $25,000 worth of editorial benefit. Here's a company with total sales and revenues of almost $120 million in fiscal 1970. I don't think 30 or 40 grand shows such a hell of a social conscience as much as it does that social involvement has certainly helped to sell magazines.

Contrast that with expenditures listed for promotion of the Big Bunny, Playboy's $5.5 million DC-9 jet: documentary film, $80,674; film coverage, $6,743; inaugural flight, air terminal party and press conference, Burbank, Calif., $3,947; jet Bunnies and costumes, $12,236; DC-9 one-shot publicity photographs, $23,047; aviation consulting services, $4,413; DC-9 press kit, $9,838; miscellaneous, $220.

Total, $141,122. This total, of course, excludes the plane's cost and any salaries involved in its operation and maintenance. It is only the promotion costs on it and not all of those, either.

Compare those two totals—$62,096 and $141,122. Is this a social-minded company? Is this a company of a highly liberal nature? Is this a company with an introspective, self-examining capacity that says to itself we are involved with the populace? If Playboy spends around 30 grand or so for social causes compared with $141,000 on just the promotion of its cockamamie plane, is it really a company with a conscience for social change? I doubt it.

I recall only one person among the top executive staff of Playboy ever espousing in private a view that showed he had a social conscience—Rosenzweig. He is a warm human being, an emotional person, and he's conscious of trauma among others. As for the others, quite to the contrary, they showed an overt lack of interest in social involvement.

All of it goes to say that the individuals who made up the corporation were another reason why the corporation was willing to spend nearly four times more on promoting a new plane than on promoting a better world.

In the following year Playboy's social conscience appeared somewhat more benevolent. The Playboy Foundation contributed about $299,000 to various causes in fiscal 1971. Playboy also contributed an undisclosed amount to the Hugh M. Hefner Foundation, a tax exempt, charitable foundation that donates to different community social services, cultural, medical and religious projects.

But still the contributions are a pittance, considering that Playboy's revenues climbed to more than $131 million in fiscal 1971, and that the total operating expenses of its mansions (in Chicago and Los Angeles) and its DC-9 jet cost it $1.9 million.

Hefner himself never misses a chance to emphasize that he is concerned about sex and drug laws and prison reform, race relations and helping the black segment of society, or supporting such causes as more day care centers for working mothers. The foundation, for instance, was a major contributor to the Masters and Johnson studies on human sexual response and continues to be a major contributor to SIECUS.

The foundation also plans to set up Help centers in major cities across the country. The first center was opened in Chicago about eight months ago. It provides an around-the-clock telephone and walk-in service to anyone troubled by problems (drugs, suicide, abortion, etc.) Help, as Hefner has explained, gives the person the feeling "he's dealing with someone sympathetic."

Another newly-formed program is the National Organization for the Reform of Marijuana Laws. Its primary purpose is aimed at repealing the marijuana laws in the U.S. The foundation is also a staunch supporter of the American Civil Liberties Union in its work in the area of invasion of privacy.

Hefner expects to become more involved in social issues personally in the future. Meanwhile, most of his money, he says, goes to the foundation's work and the foundation eventually will fall heir to almost all of the stock and profits from the entire Playboy operation.

Hefner has always felt that *Playboy* magazine has had a social impact on the magazine-reading public, but it just may be that in time to come his two foundations will have considerably more impact than the magazine ever had. With

221

his thoughts turning, as they are, to more personal involvement in social issues, that future development should please him—a foundation for immortality.

Chapter 18
It's Hefner's Party Time

The first time I went to one of Hugh Hefner's parties at the Mansion, I stayed thirty minutes; the next time fifteen minutes, and never again did I go. Whatever the rumors, and whatever people might imagine, Hefner's parties are screamingly dull—not only dull but obnoxiously loud and irritating.

Parties start usually at 10 or 10:30 at night—though he starts some at midnight—and a lot of young, single girls—secretaries, clerks and models—are invited to dress up the place. They keep a list at the Mansion of young, goodlooking girls around the city, girls who work for other companies who have been recommended by Rosenzweig's secretary, among others.

You walk into the main hall, where all the parties are held, and the bar's open and waiters are carrying drinks around, although that ends shortly after the party begins because they can't get through the crowd. If you want a drink, you go to the bar.

The staff photographers, usually David Chan and Dwight Hooker, sometimes Bill Arsenault and a couple of others, are constantly shooting photographs of the celebrities and Hefner. The strobe lights are going off because the lights are down. It's very dark except for a couple of spotlights. The strobes are almost blinding and the music is deafening. First it's recorded music and then live music by some loud rock band. Besides the young girls, certain Playboy executives and a few not-so-executives will be there.

The entire public relations staff is always there. Pat Simpson, who worked for Gottlieb, couldn't be kept away. Sometimes Irv Kupcinet, the *Chicago Sun-Times* columnist, would appear, and Mike Royko, *Chicago Daily News* columnist and author of the best seller, *Boss*, and *News* columnists Jon and Abra Anderson.

Other guests might include Gale Sayers, the Chicago Bears star, and Chet Walker of the Chicago Bulls; any visiting celebrities, actors, actresses, musicians; Robert Mitchum, Bill Cosby, Sammy Davis, Jr., Hugh O'Brien, Brock Peters, TV's Bob Crane; politicians, too, Eugene McCarthy; Jean Shrimpton, the British model—people of this ilk.

So it gets overcrowded and strobe lights are popping on and off, the music is an assault to the hearing, it is very hot, even though the air conditioning is going full blast.

Now, visualize this, you're being attacked in all your senses—your eyes ache from the strobes, your ears from the music, you're hot and sweaty, people are bumping into you, you can't get a drink because so many people are waiting, and you have to stand in a long line to get something to eat.

Why are people there?

People are there to glow in the reflection of what they feel is a star. As Hefner walks among the guests, nursing a bourbon and coke in one hand, clutching his pipe in the other, Barbi hanging on his arm, he becomes an object—not a person. In this mass of a couple hundred people, he is free to roam without the fear of personal confrontation. He is safe.

Why does Hefner invite them?

I think Hugh Hefner's idea, whether he knows it or not, is that "I am going to make it as uncomfortable as I can. I am going to attack their senses, their eyes, their ears, their bodies, and yet I will still see virtually every person I invite show up because I am Hugh Hefner and when I command people to be here, they come." It's a sop to his ego, his continuing quest for security. I think that's why he makes the parties the way he does. If he wanted, he could make them a happy medium between what they are and what they might be.

Wild orgies? The closest thing to an orgy I know of was one night the cast of "Hair" showed up and they all jumped into the swimming pool nude. What a big deal! And the next day, everybody was saying hey, did you see that, the cast of "Hair" jumped into the swimming pool nude, oh, was it wild!

At these parties, everybody looks around to see who else is there; they're all gaping, it's a typical bash. Parties are not neat, they're a sort of pain in the ass. The guests are all looking around making sure they're not missing anything. It's really funny to see how two people get together. I once saw this happen—Nelson Futch was here and Arnold Morton was over there and they're like two cobras stalking each other and at the same time looking over each other's shoulders to see what's happening.

The parties are sporadic and held usually when a major dignitary that Hefner's somehow involved with is in town. For example, the prime minister of Morocco. He threw a party in his honor because Hefner had been in Morocco to look over a possible site for a Playboy hotel and had been entertained by the P.M.

Most of the Playboy executives feel an obligation to attend these things. Preuss did not, or only rarely. I guess he had been excused after so many years, but Gottlieb was at every single one; Futch was there from start to finish; when Lownes was in town he always attended; Rosenzweig, of course, was always present. And there were always a few Bunnies, but in regular street clothes, not in their Bunny costumes.

So that's a typical Hefner party, dull, loud and obnoxious.

Now, you'd think that if Hefner throws a party like this just for the fun of it he'd really put on a show for his own birthday. Not a bit of it. In April 1970 he invited top executives to the La Costa (California) Country Club for a three-day visit and he paid the bill.

It was more than quiet, it was dull—about the most exciting thing was a special kind of shower you took after you got through the herb bath and the steam room at the spa—it was like little bullets hitting you. That was about on a par with the pedicure you had in a blacked-out room with little stars twinkling overhead. It was kind of sensuous to feel your toes being massaged when you couldn't see a thing.

Those things and a rubdown by the pool kept me interested for all of two hours and then I'd had it. The others—or some of them—played golf, but I don't like golfing so I didn't.

It was Hefner's forty-third birthday and my guess is he was thinking more about silver threads among the gold—and hating the thought of growing older—than he was about fun and games.

Except for Barbi it was a men's event—Preuss, Spectorsky, Morton, Gottlieb, Lederer, Bruder, LeRoy Neiman were all there. I went to San Francisco and then San Diego on business so I was a day late arriving. If they partied before I got there with birthday cake and champagne, I missed it. So did Preuss, I guess, because he went first to Los Angeles to transact business and then to La Costa.

The reason this insipid event was held at La Costa was because Hefner wanted to go there. He had been there once before and liked it. Anyway, we stayed in two-story duplexes, one to a man, and it was like a three-room suite, all very elegant, very nice.

The night I arrived I played gin rummy with Preuss, talked with Lederer, called my wife, read a magazine and went to sleep. (The only thing that kept me awake that long, was Preuss' constant finger-snapping during our card game. He compulsively snaps his fingers immediately after he has stubbed out a cigarette. He is unconscious of it, of course, but he never fails to do it. I became very conscious of it and ultimately decided—right or wrong, but to my own satisfaction—that this compulsion was rooted in a sense of guilt that he smoked at all, or at least as heavily as he does. I once jokingly brought it to his attention and he thought seriously that perhaps I was right. He pondered my observation—over another cigarette.) The next day Lederer and I went through the herb bath routine and we all were supposed to go on special diets. So for lunch I was handed a plate with a piece of parsley and two tiny hamburgers on it—about the size of a half-dollar—and two bites later I headed for the sandwich shop and a club sandwich. I was starved.

That was it—it was just a three-day respite, one day and two nights for me—and it was as bland as it sounds. The only ones who got any excitement or thrill out of it were the other guests, fat old people who looked on Hugh Hefner as a celebrity and gaped after him everywhere he went.

Another of Hefner's entertainments is his Sunday afternoon movies. He was always inviting me to the screenings and I always told him thanks, but I like to spend Sundays with my children, playing with the kids, which I do. But he'd look at me and say, "Oh, better things to do. I understand." He must have asked me thirty times. Sometimes I'd say, "I like to play with the kids on weekends, can I bring them?" And he'd laugh or chuckle and go a-a-ah.

As for the Sunday treat, *Time* magazine once summed up the scene as well as anybody:

"The buzz of cocktail chatter and the clink of ice cubes shrink the vast room with its monumental fireplace, paneled walls, 22-foot ceiling and two suits of medieval armor. Soft, round girls curl up with boy friends on couches beneath immense paintings by Franz Kline and Larry Rivers. The men are relaxed, confident, plainly well off. A scene straight out of *Playboy* magazine? Precisely. The men are mostly magazine employees, and the girls are some of the 24 Bunnies who room upstairs. A couple of centerfold 'Playmates', disarmingly pretty and ingenious-looking in party dresses, sip Pepsi-Cola.

"Then stillness and a turning of the heads. Down a few steps from a doorway in the corner of the room walk a man and a woman—he, casual in slacks and cardigan sweater; she, sleek in blonde hair and black dress. Simultaneously, a full-sized movie screen begins a silent descent down a side wall. Playboy Editor-Publisher Hugh Marston Hefner, 40, sinks into a love seat that has been saved for him beside the 15-foot-long stereo console. His girl friend, *Playboy* Cover Girl Mary Warren, 23, slips alongside him, puts her head on his shoulder. A butler brings a bowl of hot buttered popcorn and bottles of Pepsi; the lights dim; the movie begins . . ."

Except for Hefner's age (now 45), the girl who puts her head on his shoulder (now Barbi) and the particular movie shown each Sunday, the above scene hasn't changed since *Time* described it back in March of 1967. I doubt if it ever will.

Chapter 19
Lobbying For The Lobby

In 1965, Playboy acquired a 63-year leasehold on the 37-story former Palmolive Building for the sum of $2,700,000, giving Playboy control of the entire building. The venerable structure is situated just three blocks from Lake Michigan at the corner of the exclusive North Michigan Avenue district and is surrounded by fancy hotels, shops and restaurants. It is one-half block east of the former location of the Chicago Playboy Club and a stone's throw from the high-rise, high-rent section of Lake Shore Drive known as the "Gold Coast."

Although dwarfed by the 100-story John Hancock Building down the block, the Playboy Building stands a respectable 408 feet high from street level. Rising an additional 90 feet or so atop the building is a rotating searchlight, dubbed the "Bunny Beacon" by the Chicago press. The beam can be seen from the ground as far as 80 miles away and more than 250 miles by air. The beacon is serviced by two full-time electricians and annual cost for upkeep and power amounts to more than $30,000. So stands the Playboy monument, in utter awe of itself, an unparalled fantasy factory.

While on the outside the structural steel, garbed in Bedford stone, gives the Playboy Building a stately look reminiscent of the Sullivan school of architecture, the interior—especially the Playboy offices—is something else. Approximately two-thirds, or ten floors, of the building's 340,000 square feet of rentable office space is occupied by Playboy and includes its executive and editorial offices. The entire complex was put together for a tidy $2 million.

Each of the floors has its own departmental reception area, which is reached directly from six elevators. There is always a young, attractive receptionist who complements the area's design unity of contoured panels and free-flowing curves. The receptionist's desk, with its thick marble top and solid walnut casework, is typical of Playboy's overall furniture design. Tweedy Spicepoint carpeting covers the floors and homespun copper-colored fabric covers all reception chairs, clustered around a circular knee-high table adorned with several issues of *Playboy*.

Soft incandescent lights scooped out of sand-finished, sculptured walls and niches blend from ceiling to floor, providing a constant color background for the original pieces of editorial art that hang on the walls throughout the offices. The office area is reached via one of several passageways, their truncated, recessed fluorescent lighting illuminating more *Playboy* illustrations.

The corridors open into a secretarial pool area flanked by the offices of the various department personnel. The typical office follows a more conventional pattern. There is mood lighting; custom-designed desks with marble tops and oiled walnut casework, and at least one wall covered floor to ceiling with heavy dark cork for tacking up memos, notes, centerfolds, whatever. Tracked casement draperies of mohair and linen are pocketed into the ceiling above special walnut casework at the window level.

It was a big and flashy move from Playboy's previous offices—a four-story building and four annexes nearby on East Ohio Street on Chicago's Near North Side—occupied from 1956 until the 1966 move into the new building.

The only part of the Playboy Building that had remained dated was its once elegant and spacious main-floor lobby, dominated by walnut-paneled walls and marble floors. That is now all changed. But it was the silly, fiddle-faddling around, the circumstances prior to the change, that most fascinated me. That, and the fact that I got so involved in it, and finally, the specific happening that revealed so much about the character and motives of one particular executive.

One morning my phone rang and Arnold Morton said, "Steve, I'd like you to come down to the old conference room to see something."

And there, approximately half the size of the real thing, is a model for the new lobby. It's something out of 1953, a nothing sort of a design. The floor is covered with an orange carpet, the walls are white, the pillars, the structural supports, are covered in walnut, and that's all.

I looked at this and walked around it and didn't say a word, and Arnold said, "Well, what do you think?"

"What do I think?" I said. "I think it's a waste of the $15,000 I understand you paid for this travesty."

"Oh? Why do you say that?" Arnold asked.

"Because all it is is an empty space, Arnold," I told him. "It's a space people can walk through and that is all you've accomplished. You could have done that for a lot less than $15,000 by simply a description saying we're going to take out everything but the pillars and we're going to paint the walls white, install an orange carpet and cover the pillars with walnut and that would have served the purpose."

And at that Arnold absolutely blew up and he said, "Well, let me tell you something, it's better than that thing you put together, you and your artforms," and he started poking me in the chest with his index finger, "this is what Hefner likes and that's why I've done it."

"Arnold," I said, "you spent $15,000 because this is what you think Hefner likes? You spent fifteen grand because this is what you think will appeal to him without any thought for whether it is good?"

"Let me tell you something," he said, poking my chest all the while, "if I were you I wouldn't mess with the man, because this is what the man likes and this is what I am going to give him and if you're smart you'll listen to me and you won't mess with the man either."

"Why is that, Arnold?" I asked him.

"Because I am too goddamn old, I am almost a grandfather. I am too old to start looking for a job now and unless you want to go looking for a job you better wise up to this right now."

I walked out.

The subject of a lobby design had been under review long before I joined Playboy. The idea was to move the Chicago club to the new Playboy building and the lobby was to serve the club, the hotel and the offices in the building.

But nobody could ever get together on a lobby design because nobody could read Hefner's mind closely enough to determine what he really wanted. One month there would be a walnut and white tile lobby; another an earth-tones approach; another a futuristic architectural concept—all because Hefner had been heard to say at one time or another that he liked them.

Once, somebody got the idea of doing the lobby as the inside of the Big Bunny, because Hefner was supposed to have been very thrilled with the magnificence of the jet. So that was put together and Hefner suddenly blurted that he "hated the inside of the plane, thought it looked cheap and garish and stupid and wanted the entire thing torn out and redone." (It was, at a cost of a half-million dollars.)

Ted Rogers came up with an approach. Talking in his favorite words, he said, "I want this to be an AV (audio-visual) concept where you walk in and every sense is hit by this spectacular of sound and sight and feeling and sensation." And he was going to hire a New York communications consulting firm to implement his idea.

Now, these experts make like witch doctors and they carry their drums around with them to different offices and they speak of AV boogie men and say things like, "If you won't go along with our audio-visual concepts your mother is going to die." Really, this is so!

They told Rogers that for $285,000 they would create an audio-visual screen of 16 television monitors. When all the verbiage is set aside, it comes out to be 16 TV cameras that will then cost $30,000 a month to program and what you have is a cacophony of sound and sight going on all at once. On a 25-by-40-foot wall you're going to have 16 TV monitors, each showing a different thing or perhaps two the same thing. You'll see one TV monitor showing what's going on in the club and another talking about what's new in Chicago today and another showing a panorama of Michigan Avenue and so on.

There were some positives to it but not enough to justify more than a half-million dollars the first year and $350,000 a year thereafter. And all this did for the lobby was take up one section of the wall and there was still the rest of the area, for which a total expenditure of a half-million dollars had been allocated.

So that was Rogers' solution and Hefner didn't even respond, he didn't say a word, he just ordered a pork chop sandwich.

That was when I started putting together a lobby concept, based on our objective, on what we were trying to accomplish. First, we had to enable people to get to the club, to the hotel, to the offices; then, to provide them with information about Playboy the corporation, because this is the world headquarters; to provide them with information to implement whatever it is they intended to do when they came into the place, buy a drink or rent a room or see somebody or whatever.

To accomplish those things was relatively easy except for expressing what Playboy is. I started thinking of all the different manifestations of the organization. I then decided to have an outside architectural consultant render into plans what it would look like.

I was in the process of putting this together when Arnold Morton looked at it and said, "Hefner will never go for it."

"Why not?" I asked.

"Because it doesn't have earth tones," he said.

That's when he decided to do a new lobby approach himself and that was the one-to-two scale model he showed me that cost $15,000.

When he said to me "you and your artforms," he was referring to the fact that I had planned to commission Red Grooms, the New York sculptor who did the construction called "Chicago" that the Art Institute exhibited for several years. In fact, I had already secured Grooms' agreement to a commission for a construction in the center of the lobby through which people would actually walk. It was to be a respresentation of Playboy Enterprises, showing all of its manifold parts and how they related.

I felt this was a way of saying "here's not just a sign-post showing the magazine, the hotels, the clubs, the transportation service, upcoming foreign editions, the book club and so on, but a statement that Playboy is a lot more than most people think."

Similar to the construction of "Chicago," as you were going through it you could touch things and some part of the construction would be moving slightly. It was involving, it was artful, it had class to it.

But Hefner never saw it.

Chapter 20
And Then There Was One

It was the fall of 1970.

Things were happening. Changes were going on at Playboy, not only in the direct-mail marketing area but in corporate development, the advertising and public relations areas, in promotion and hotel and key sales efforts. The changes were positive, resulting in growth.

I even sensed a change in Hefner's attitude toward new approaches to the traditional ideas that Playboy had clung to since its inception. The ice began cracking back in June of 1970 at the Las Vegas sales convention when Hefner grudgingly went along with the newly designed Christmas ads. Now, I was on my way to the Mansion to do battle with Hefner again; to try pursuading him to agree to yet another change. This time it dealt with a series of ads called "What Sort of Man Reads *Playboy*?" The series had been running for about fourteen years in the front of the magazine and had become the butt of satires and jokes because it was dated.

Hefner always wanted to see every "What Sort of Man Reads *Playboy*?" ad before its actual implementation into the magazine. He apparently had created the original ads.

The existing format featured a man with one young woman being ogled by another young woman. This situation was supposed to say to the advertiser of a product or service that *Playboy* had a great audience for his offering. It was also supposed to convince the reader that he could attract that kind of admiration because he read *Playboy* and used products or services advertised in it.

I disagreed with the approach because it was hackneyed; it had become so trite over the years that the purposes of the ad were not being achieved.

After studying the existing ads, I decided that the camera, instead of focusing upon the scene, should focus upon the main characters, the man in the company of the girl, emphasizing her adoration of him, his strength of character and so on. I omitted the female adoring from afar because the highest form of adoration is not the gaze of a passing female—who may just be myopic and not adoring at all—but the relationship between one female and one male. Each of the eight new ads incorporated an inset scene of the terrain, or the environment, that enabled us finally to tell, in very short order, a pictorial story.

I recommended that we do a test, or a sort of readership study that would show how many people saw each of the two ads—the old and the new—and their reaction to each.

The first time I presented the ads, as expected, the response was negative. Rosenzweig sent me a memo stating that Hefner was displeased with the ads because they didn't capture what "Hef" wanted to convey about the man who reads *Playboy*. So, I requested a meeting with Hefner.

About a week before I was to meet with him, Hefner sent me a memo, chastising me for taking too long to submit a new design for the Bunny costume, as though time were the criterion for success.

It had been three months since I had taken over the project. I had commissioned five designers—Donald Brooks, the well-known fashion designer; two in California and two in New York who had designed costumes for Broadway plays.

One of these was Madame Bertha, a 78-year-old fat lady, who had submitted the best design of all. It was a diaphanous top over a bra type of affair, an overall pant and top under this diaphanous covering. It was a very sexy outfit that she had sketched, yet it wasn't at all revealing. I thought it was the essence of what the costume should be—suggestive and provocative, but not naked.

The thing that really bothered me about the memo, however, was its overtones. Hefner had never before shown any impatience with me. In fact, he had never before prodded. But now came this sudden outburst. I didn't know what to make of it.

But on Friday, October 29—the day of our meeting— Bunny costumes and lobby designs were the farthest things from my mind. My immediate concern was with "What Sort of Man Reads *Playboy*?" I was trying to anticipate what Hefner's specific criticisms would be and how I would counter them. It was a mild, sunny afternoon; a day that couldn't have been more pleasant. Neither could the conditions under which Hefner and I were to meet—at least for me. Rosenzweig and Preuss were not going to be at the meeting and that pleased me. I had learned not to look to them for anything contributory. Their passiveness had only become interference. I was going to talk to Hefner on a one-to-one basis, as we had that afternoon in Las Vegas.

When I arrived at the Mansion I felt confident. Hefner greeted me cordially in the conference room and we began.

"Huf, I realize you have been very close to these ads for years and are pleased with them. But I think the format needs to be changed by using stronger graphics and stronger copy. I feel these ads are a better rendering of what *Playboy* is trying to say to both the advertiser and reader."

I paused, glancing at Hefner's face for some expression that would possibly convey his feelings about what I was saying. He was rather solemn, his face almost expressionless. I continued my presentation, but Hefner's apathy was too distracting. His mind seemed to be wandering. He was lighting his pipe a little more frequently and evading my glance.

237

He was sort of not there. He appeared to be daydreaming.

"What's up, Huf? I have the feeling that something is on your mind instead of 'What Kind of Man Reads *Playboy*?' Is there something you want to talk to me about?"

He puffed on his pipe, lit it once more, and said, "Yes, there is something I want to talk to you about."

"I think it's going to come out whether I ask you to talk about it or not," I said, "so why don't you tell me what it is."

He took the pipe from his mouth, looked straight at me, and said:

"I can't take it any longer, you've been a continuous frustration to me. For seventeen years I haven't had to answer to anyone, but for the last year I have had to answer to you. I don't like that feeling of personal frustration." He went back to his pipe.

"Well," I said, "I'm also very frustrated in dealing with you for the very reason that you *don't* recognize the need to answer to other people. The only way this company is going to be here seventeen years from now is if you allow there to develop a group of people to whom you feel a need to answer."

Hefner thought for a moment and then replied, "Perhaps you're right but I won't accept the frustration that comes of it. However right you are, it will have to be done another way because I won't permit this personal frustration to continue."

At that point I was faced with just two alternatives. I could back down, promising to fall in line with the other Playboy executives, to be a "good boy" thereafter. Or I could continue the conversation in the obvious direction it was heading. There was really no choice.

"Are you implying that one of us is going to leave this company?" I asked.

Hefner drew several short and furious puffs on his pipe, smiled and said, "Yes, that's right."

"I have a feeling that it isn't you."

"Yes, I think you're right again," he said, still smiling.

"I have the feeling that I'm the one that's leaving."

238

"Correct," Hefner nodded.

"Ok," I said. I stood up, shook hands with him and walked out of the conference room.

On my way back to the office I couldn't help wondering at what point Hefner became aware of the frustration I was causing him. Was it during the period when I was cleaning out the deadwood in personnel? For the first five people, or ten or perhaps fifteen, maybe everything was fine. He recognized that if those people were going, there must be a reason for it. They weren't needed if they weren't being replaced.

But at some point, Hefner probably started to have a negative reaction. He must have said to himself: "Wait a minute, I'm the head of this company. I personally hired some of these people Byer is letting go. I've allowed them to stay here all this time. Now, if he's right, does that make me wrong?"

Or was his frustration building up change by change? Programs that he created were being changed. But to get him to go along with the changes, whether they were in the product line or a new advertising approach, was a painstaking and pressuring proposition. I was always pushing. But that's precisely what it took.

Then it dawned upon me—that memo on the costumes. Perhaps it was Hefner's way of saying, "I can push, too." Or as preposterous as it may seem, maybe there is no place for a marketing director at Playboy. There have been six marketing directors in the past five years . . .

When I got back to the office there was a call from Preuss waiting for me. I unloosened my tie, walked down the four flights to his office and went in, closing the door.

"For Christ's sake, why did you do it?" he asked.

"I didn't do it," I said. And that was true, I hadn't done it. I simply realized that if it didn't happen now it would happen six months from now or two months or a week or two years from now. It had to happen, because of the nature of the individual.

"But why did you let it get to that point, you could have stopped it," Preuss said.

"No," I said, "I couldn't have stopped it, that's the way it was happening."

"Why the hell didn't you reconcile with him?" Preuss asked. "Why didn't you tell him you were sorry, that you wouldn't do that anymore, or something to that effect?"

"There was nothing to reconcile," I said, "he has one view of this company and I have another, he owns the stock and I don't."

"I just don't believe it," Preuss said, "you could have reconciled it so easily and you should have."

"Look," I said, "why don't we work out the details of my departure, because it's here—"

And we did.